Wow! Smart Vocabulary

4

집필진: 김미희, E·NEXT 영어연구회
김미희, 박경희, 박소현, 임지연, 홍정민, 한성욱, Christina KyungJin Ham, Leeanne Madden(Editorial Advisor)

김미희 선생님은 이화여자대학교 영어교육과를 졸업하고 EBS English에서 방영하는 'Yo! Yo! Play Time'과 'EBS 방과후 영어'를 집필 및 검토하셨으며, 베스트셀러인 '10시간 영문법'과 '영어 글쓰기왕 비법 따라잡기' 등의 많은 영어교재를 집필하셨습니다. E·NEXT 영어연구회는 김미희 선생님을 중심으로, 세계 영어교육의 흐름에 발맞추어 효과적이고 바람직한 영어 교수·학습 방법을 연구하는 영어교육 전문가들의 모임입니다.

Smart Vocabulary ④

지은이 김미희
펴낸이 정규도
펴낸곳 다락원

초판 1쇄 발행 2011년 11월 17일
초판 7쇄 인쇄 2023년 12월 21일

편집장 최주연
책임편집 장경희, 오승현
영문교정 Michael A. Putlack
아트디렉터 정현석
디자인 윤미주, 김은미, 이승현

다락원 경기도 파주시 문발로 211
전화: (02)736-2031 내선 251~252
Fax: (02)732-2037
출판등록 1977년 9월 16일 제406-2008-000007호

값 9,500원

ISBN 978-89-277-4028-5
      978-89-277-4030-8(set)

http://www.darakwon.co.kr
다락원 홈페이지를 통해 책 속의 영문 해석 자료,
표제어 및 스토리 MP3 파일을 받아 보실 수 있습니다.

출간에 도움 주신 분들

신가윤(Brown International School 국제학교 분당캠퍼스 원장)
배정연(키다리교육센터 메인 강사)
Jeniffer Kim(English Hunters 원장)
전남숙(KidsCollege 원장)
Leigh Stella Lage(성남외국어고등학교 원어민교사)
조은정(아이스펀지 잉글리쉬 원감)
심희선 이영란 박종희
이선옥(OK's Class 원장)
박혜정(잉글루 고창 어학원 원장)

내지일러스트 정민경   표지일러스트 노유이

WOW! Smart Vocabulary를 추천합니다!

단어 공부는 외국어 공부의 기본이자 실력입니다. 단어 공부에 대한 의견이 분분하지만, 영어를 제 2외국어로 삼고 있는 우리 어린이들에게 단어 학습이 필요하다는 사실은 부정할 수 없습니다. 문제는 방법이지요. 단어의 철자와 뜻만 외우는 것은 너무 단편적이어서 큰 의미가 없습니다. 어린이들이 쉽고 재미있게 단어를 익히면서 실생활에서 활용할 수 있는 효과적인 단어 학습 방법이 필요합니다. 그런 의미에서, 기계적인 암기에서 끝나지 않고 꼭 필요한 단어들을 이야기 속에서 익힐 수 있는 WOW! Smart Vocabulary 시리즈를 적극 추천합니다.

김정렬 (한국교원대학교 영어교육과 교수, 초등영어교과서 저자, 한국초등영어교육학회 회장)

제시된 단어를 문제 풀이를 통해 이해 수준을 확인하던 기존의 어휘 학습 방법을 탈피하여, 학습자가 관심을 가질 수 있는 다양한 주제의 어휘들을 논픽션과 픽션으로 이루어진 스토리와 연계해서 자연스럽게 학습할 수 있는 점이 WOW! Smart Vocabulary 시리즈의 가장 큰 특징이라고 할 수 있습니다. 또한 워크북은 배운 단어들을 스스로 정리하고 확실히 익히는 데 매우 효과적인 문제 유형들로 이루어져 있네요.

샤이니 김재영 (EBS English 영어방송진행자)

단어를 많이 아는 것도 중요하지만 실제 생활에서 상황에 맞는 단어를 활용하는 것이 더욱 중요합니다. 같은 단어라 할지라도 때론 문장 속에서 여러 의미로 해석되기도 하고, 다른 뜻으로 쓰여지기도 합니다. WOW! Smart Vocabulary 시리즈는 초등학교에서 중학교까지 단계적으로 단어를 학습할 수 있도록 구성되어 있으며, 스토리 속에서 살아 움직이는 단어를 익혀 실제 생활에 활용할 수 있도록 전략적으로 구성되어 있어 재미와 지식, 단어의 실제적 활용을 동시에 잡는 단어 교재라고 여겨집니다.

조은옥 (성지초등학교 교감, 초등영어교과서 저자)

한 주제별로 논픽션, 픽션의 두 가지 레슨이 짝으로 이루어진 점이 아주 신선하네요. 또한 스토리 속에 학습 단어들을 적용해 가며 나의 단어를 만들어 갈 수 있게 해주는 구성도 마음에 듭니다. Unit마다 쉬운 단어부터 난이도 있는 단어 학습까지 할 수 있어서 학습자가 성취감을 느낌과 동시에 난이도 있는 단어에도 도전 정신을 갖도록 해주는 것이 이 책의 큰 매력입니다.

이수진 (코너스톤 국제학교 아카데믹매니저)

WOW! Smart Vocabulary 시리즈는 초등학교뿐 아니라 중학교 수준의 필수 어휘까지 주제에 맞게 학습할 수 있습니다. 단순히 뜻을 외우거나 어휘의 기능에만 초점을 두는 학습이 아니라 어휘의 문법적인 쓰임과 실용적인 표현을 통한 문장 활용까지 배울 수 있게 구성한 것이 좋습니다. 더 나아가 스토리 속에서 어휘를 익힘으로써 어휘 교재이면서도 어휘 수준을 능가하는 의미 있는 학습을 제공한다는 점이 큰 장점이라고 할 수 있습니다. 또한 효율적인 연습 문제 유형들도 돋보입니다.

박진희 (중탑초등학교 교사)

WOW! Smart Vocabulary has various nonfiction and fiction stories which give this book its charm. These interesting stories will keep students motivated. Along with engaging exercises, students are sure to efficiently learn new words from this book.

Janet Y Ko (용마초등학교 원어민 교사)

이 책의 구성과 특징

WOW! Smart Vocabulary에는 여러 영어 교육 전문가 선생님들이
오랜 시간 동안 현장에서 직접 적용해보고 지도해본 실제 경험이 고스란히 녹아 들어가 있습니다.
모든 Unit은 하나의 주제 아래 Nonfiction과 Fiction이라는
두 개의 쌍둥이 Lesson으로 이루어져 있습니다.
첫 번째 Lesson에서는 실화, 신문기사, 광고 등과 같이
사실적인 정보를 주는 이야기(Nonfiction)를 통해 단어들을 익힙니다.
두 번째 Lesson에서는 주인공과 함께 친구가 되어
가상의 이야기(Fiction) 속에 빠져들면서 단어를 배우게 됩니다.

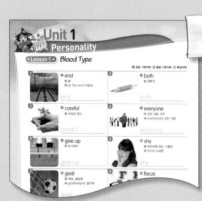

표제어 + 빈칸에 써 보기

주제에 따라 서로 연관성이 있는 표제어들을 제시하기 때문에 기억하기
쉽습니다. 사진이나 삽화를 통해 각 단어의 분명한 의미를 바로 파악할
수 있고, 시각적 연상을 통해 단어를 감각적으로 기억할 수 있습니다.

※단어 선정과 분류는 교육부 개정교육과정 기본어휘 목록표를 바탕으
로 했으며, 이 외에도 실제 초등학생의 일상생활에서 친숙한 단어와 중학
영어 학습을 위해 꼭 알아두어야 할 단어까지 함께 제시했습니다.

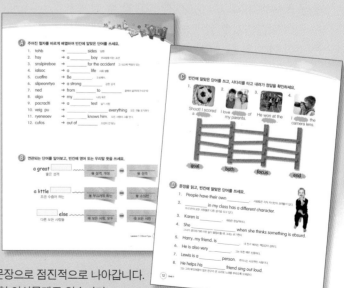

단계적인 연습문제

단계적인 연습문제 풀이를 통해 단어에서 구로, 구에서 문장으로 점진적으로 나아갑니다.
학습하는 단어와 관련하여 기억하기 쉽게 도와주는 확장형 연상문제도 있습니다.
단어의 철자만 익히는 것이 아니라, 그 단어가 문장 속에서 어떻게 쓰이는지 학습할 수 있습니다.

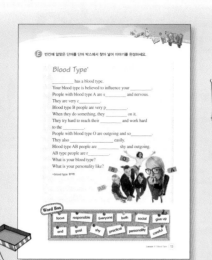

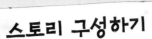

스토리 구성하기

각 Lesson의 마지막 단계는 Lesson에서 제시하는
학습단어들로 스토리를 만드는 것입니다.
논픽션과 픽션의 재미있는 쌍둥이 스토리 속에
녹아 있는 학습단어를 찾아 쓰면서,
배운 단어들이 실제 스토리 속에서
어떻게 살아 움직이는지 경험해 봅니다.

별책부록 - 워크북

본 책의 각 Unit에서 배운 학습단어의 우리말 뜻을 써 보며 스스로 실력을 체크하고,
각 Lesson마다 등장하는 스토리 속 문장을 통해 다시 한번 학습단어를 점검합니다.
이어지는 Review Test에서는 단어의 단순 암기가 아닌 실용적인 활용에 중점을 두고 구성한
다양한 유형의 문제들을 풀어보면서 실력을 확인해 봅니다.

학습 예시

WOW! Smart Vocabulary는 총 5권으로 구성되어 있고,
권 당 10개의 Unit, 한 Unit에 두 개의 Lesson이 들어있습니다.
한 Lesson을 학습하는 데 약 한 시간이 걸리므로,
한 Unit을 대체로 두 시간 동안 학습할 수 있습니다.
WOW! Smart Vocabulary를 일주일에 5시간 학습할 경우
권 당 4주, 총 5개월 정도가 소요됩니다.

	학습 시간	Unit / Lesson	표제어 수 & 비율	Total
1권	20시간 Lesson 당 1시간	10/20	Unit별 20개(Lesson별 10개) 교육부 제시 초등 기본어휘 70~80% / 중등 기본어휘 + 확장어휘 20~30%	200
2권	20시간 Lesson 당 1시간	10/20	Unit별 20개(Lesson별 10개) 교육부 제시 초등 기본어휘 60~70% / 중등 기본어휘 + 확장어휘 30~40%	200
3권	20시간 Lesson 당 1시간	10/20	Unit별 24개(Lesson별 12개) 교육부 제시 초등 기본어휘 50~60% / 중등 기본어휘 + 확장어휘 40~50%	240
4권	20시간 Lesson 당 1시간	10/20	Unit별 24개(Lesson별 12개) 교육부 제시 초등 기본어휘 40~50% / 중등 기본어휘 + 확장어휘 50~60%	240
5권	20시간 Lesson 당 1시간	10/20	Unit별 28개(Lesson별 14개) 교육부 제시 초등 기본어휘 30~40% / 중등 기본어휘 + 확장어휘 60~70%	280
총 학습단어 수				1,160

4권 단어구성표

4권		초등 기본어휘	중등 기본어휘	확장 어휘	표제어 수
Unit 1 Personality	Lesson 1 Blood Type	end, both, careful, everyone, give up	shy, goal, focus, social, practical, personality, responsible		24
	Lesson 2 New Classmates	kid, like, answer, others, classmate	awful, tease, tough, borrow, selfish, complain	naughty	
Unit 2 A Swimming Race	Lesson 1 A Freestyle Swimming Race	that, second, take place, do one's best, catch up with, neck and neck	block, record, result, signal, predict, powerfully		24
	Lesson 2 Turtle, the Lifesaver	left, than, go back, run away	save, toward, anymore, lifesaver	paddle, splash, turtle, get a cramp	
Unit 3 The Tallest Building	Lesson 1 Skyscraper	city, tall, strong, company, welcome	steel, height, million, observation	sway, skyline, skyscraper	24
	Lesson 2 The Tower of Babel	into, floor, stone, quickly	dust, brick, order, storm, heaven, destroy, collapse	tornado	
Unit 4 Paper World	Lesson 1 Papyrus	no, ago, then, wetland, sunlight	part, sheet, strip, origin, ancient, century	soak	24
	Lesson 2 Magic Drawing Paper	erase, listen, sketch, art class, drawing paper, look around, give out light	rub, wave, realize, everything	pop out	
Unit 5 Water Changes	Lesson 1 The Water Cycle	or, up, down, river	heat, flow, form, rise, surface	water drop, water cycle, water vapor	24
	Lesson 2 A Wonderful Experience	cool, cover, sheep, person	ocean, a lot of, freeze, lighten, turn into	chilly, evaporate, each other	

4권		초등 기본어휘	중등 기본어휘	확장 어휘	표제어 수
Unit 6 **About Junk Food**	Lesson 1 Fast Food	as, test, movie, weight, throw up	meal, limit, offer, distance, depression, treatment	quit	24
	Lesson 2 Burger Fighting	hate, fresh, today, woman, way, fall under a spell	human, regret, remove, already, friendship	snatch	
Unit 7 **The Seven Stars**	Lesson 1 The Big Dipper	once, round, almost	bowl, sailor, describe, northern, position, direction	ox, wagon, constellation	24
	Lesson 2 Orion and the Scorpion	alone, never, night	bite, leave, sword, attack, bother, opposite, southern, boastful	coward	
Unit 8 **Famous Places**	Lesson 1 The Moai on Easter Island	and, how, heavy, number	bottom, discover, research, attractive	carve, statue, sleigh, heritage	24
	Lesson 2 Nick at the Pyramid	loud, speak, watch, field trip, black out	exit, occur, backward, exhibition, come up to	scared, mummy	
Unit 9 **A Mysterious Plant**	Lesson 1 The Venus Flytrap	if, poor, wide, short, endanger, greenhouse	allow, mysterious	crawl, digest, unlike, nutrient	24
	Lesson 2 A Helpful Plant	die, key, side, helpful, lose one's footing	gather, solution, troublesome, get rid of	swamp, shovel, tickle	
Unit 10 **The Guinness Book**	Lesson 1 A Guinness World Record	now, who, send	fact, huge, detail, measure, apply, break a record	dwarf, cockroach, the same ~ as …	24
	Lesson 2 Nick's World Record	tie, beef, chalk, continue, in class, fall off, button up	sore, blame, upset, medicine, disappoint		

Contents

Unit 1 **Personality**
Lesson 1 Blood Type
Lesson 2 New Classmates

Unit 2 **A Swimming Race**
Lesson 1 A Freestyle Swimming Race
Lesson 2 Turtle, the Lifesaver

Unit 3 **The Tallest Building**
Lesson 1 Skyscraper
Lesson 2 The Tower of Babel

Unit 4 **Paper World**
Lesson 1 Papyrus
Lesson 2 Magic Drawing Paper

Unit 5 **Water Changes**
Lesson 1 The Water Cycle
Lesson 2 A Wonderful Experience

Unit 6 **About Junk Food**
Lesson 1 Fast Food
Lesson 2 Burger Fighting

Unit 7 **The Seven Stars**
Lesson 1 The Big Dipper
Lesson 2 Orion and the Scorpion

Unit 8 **Famous Places**
Lesson 1 The Moai on Easter Island
Lesson 2 Nick at the Pyramid

Unit 9 **A Mysterious Plant**
Lesson 1 The Venus Flytrap
Lesson 2 A Helpful Plant

Unit 10 **The Guinness Book**
Lesson 1 A Guinness World Record
Lesson 2 Nick's World Record

Wow! Smart Vocabulary

4

Unit 1
Personality

 초등 기본어휘  중등 기본어휘 ◎ 확장어휘

1
☆ **end**
🅟 끝
🅚 at the end 마침내

end

2
☆ **both**
🅗 양쪽의

both

3
☆ **careful**
🅗 조심성 있는

careful

4
☆ **everyone**
🅓 모든 사람, 모두
🅤 everybody 모든 사람

everyone

5
☆ **give up**
🅚 포기하다

give up

6
◇ **shy**
🅗 부끄러워 하는, 수줍은
🅤 timid 소심한

shy

7
◇ **goal**
🅟 목표, 결승점
🅟 goalkeeper 골키퍼

goal

8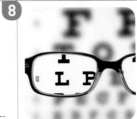
◇ **focus**
🅔 초점을 맞추다
🅟 초점
🅚 focus on ~에 집중하다

focus

9
◇ **social**
🅗 사회적인, 사교적인
🅤 friendly 사교적인

social

10
◇ **practical**
🅗 실용적인, 현실적인

practical

11
◇ **personality**
🅟 성격, 개성
🅤 character 성격
🅟 person 사람

personality

12
◇ **responsible**
🅗 책임이 있는, 책임감 있는
🅟 responsibility 책임

responsible

 주어진 철자를 바르게 배열하여 빈칸에 알맞은 단어를 쓰세요.

1. tohb → _____ sides 양면
2. hsy → a _____ boy 부끄럼을 타는 소년
3. snslpireboe → _____ for the accident 그 사고에 책임이 있는
4. ialsoc → a _____ life 사회 생활
5. cuaflre → Be _____. 조심하라.
6. slipeonrtya → a strong _____ 강한 성격
7. ned → from _____ to _____ 끝에서 끝까지(구석구석)
8. algo → my _____ 나의 목표
9. pacraclti → a _____ test 실기 시험
10. veig pu → _____ _____ everything 모든 것을 포기하다
11. ryeneoev → _____ knows him. 모든 사람이 그를 안다.
12. cufos → out of _____ 초점이 안 맞는

B 연관되는 단어를 알아보고, 빈칸에 영어 또는 우리말 뜻을 쓰세요.

a great _____
좋은 성격
〜 _____ 명 성격, 개성 = _____ 명 성격

a little _____
조금 수줍어 하는
〜 _____ 형 부끄러워 하는 = _____ 형 소심한

_____ else
다른 모든 사람들
〜 _____ 대 모든 사람, 모두 = _____ 대 모든 사람

C 빈칸에 알맞은 단어를 쓰고, 사다리를 타고 내려가 정답을 확인하세요.

1.
Shoot! I scored a _____.

2.
I love _____ of my parents.

3.
He won in the _____.

4.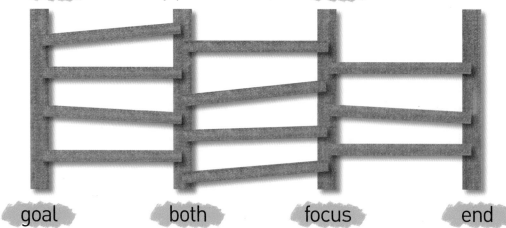
I _____ the camera lens.

| goal | both | focus | end |

D 문장을 읽고, 빈칸에 알맞은 단어를 쓰세요.

1. People have their own _____.   사람들은 각자 자신만의 성격들이 있다.

2. _____ in my class has a different character.
우리 반의 모든 사람들은 다른 성격을 갖고 있다.

3. Karen is _____.   캐런은 현실적이다.

4. She _____ _____ when she thinks something is absurd.
그녀가 생각하기에 어떤 일이 불합리할 때 그녀는 포기한다.

5. Harry, my friend, is _____.   내 친구 해리는 책임감이 강하다.

6. He is also very _____.   그는 또한 매우 신중하다.

7. Lewis is a _____ person.   루이스는 사교적인 사람이다.

8. He helps his _____ friend sing out loud.
그는 그의 부끄러움이 많은 친구가 큰 소리로 노래를 부르도록 도와준다.

 빈칸에 알맞은 단어를 단어 박스에서 찾아 넣어 이야기를 완성하세요.

Blood Type*

_____ has a blood type.

Your blood type is believed to influence your _____.

People with blood type A are s_____ and nervous.

They are very c_____.

Blood type B people are very p_____.

When they do something, they _____ on it.

They try hard to reach their _____ and work hard to the _____.

People with blood type O are outgoing and so_____.

They also _____ _____ easily.

Blood type AB people are _____ shy and outgoing.

AB type people are r_____.

What is your blood type?

What is your personality like?

＊blood type 혈액형

Word Box

focus   responsible   Everyone   both   social   give up

end   goal   shy   practical   personality   careful

New Classmates

1

★ **kid**
명 아이, 어린이
반 adult 어른, 성인

kid

2

★ **like**
동 좋아하다 전 ~ 같이, ~처럼
반 dislike 싫어하다
구 feel like ~하고 싶다

like

3

★ **answer**
동 대답하다
명 대답
반 ask 물어보다

answer

4

◇ **others**
명 다른 것들, 다른 사람들

others

5

★ **classmate**
명 반 친구, 급우
유 friend 친구

classmate

6

◇ **awful**
형 끔찍한, 지독한, 무서운
유 horrible 무서운, 끔찍한

awful

7

◇ **tease**
동 놀리다, 괴롭히다

tease

8

◇ **tough**
형 거친, 힘든, 질긴

tough

9

◇ **borrow**
동 빌리다
반 lend 빌려주다

borrow

10

◇ **selfish**
형 이기적인
명 self 자기 자신

selfish

11

◇ **complain**
동 불평하다

complain

12

◎ **naughty**
형 개구쟁이의, 장난이 심한

naughty

A 주어진 철자를 바르게 배열하여 빈칸에 알맞은 단어를 쓰세요.

1. dik → a smart _____ 똑똑한 아이
2. ikle → _____ that 저것처럼
3. htrseo → think of _____ 다른 사람들을 생각하다
4. casslatem → an elementary school _____ 초등학교 반 친구
5. aswern → give an _____ 대답을 하다
6. coplamin → Don't _____. 불평하지 마라.
7. oghut → a _____ guy 거친 남자
8. afulw → an _____ test 끔찍한 시험
9. elsihsf → a _____ woman 이기적인 여자
10. nagtyhu → a _____ boy 개구쟁이 소년
11. owborr → _____ a book 책을 빌리다
12. eseat → _____ someone about their appearance
그들의 외모에 대해 놀리다

B 다음 장면에 어울리는 단어를 보기에서 골라 넣어 문장을 완성하세요.

| kids | classmates | naughty | tease |

1. Look at those _____ .
2. They look like _____ .
3. They _____ a girl about her hairstyle.
4. They are really _____ .

C 문장을 읽고, 빈칸에 알맞은 뜻을 쓴 후 해당하는 것을 선으로 연결하세요.

동 좋아하다 •

전 ~ 같이, ~처럼 •

like

Go!

전 ~하고 싶은 •

• I can't swim <u>like</u> you.
  나는 너_____ 수영할 수가 없다.

• I <u>like</u> you.
  나는 너를 _____.

• My dad feels <u>like</u> dancing.
  우리 아빠는 춤추고 _____.

D 문장을 읽고, 빈칸에 알맞은 단어를 쓰세요.

1. Today, I have a new _____, Janet. She is my new partner.
   오늘, 나는 새로운 반 친구인 쟈넷을 만난다. 그녀는 내 새 짝꿍이다.

2. It is _____ for me.   그것은 나에게 끔찍하다.

3. Because I think she is _____.   왜냐하면 나는 그녀가 이기적이라고 생각하기 때문이다.

4. Someone tried to _____ a pencil from her yesterday.
   어제 누군가가 그녀에게서 연필을 빌리려고 했었다.

5. Someone asked her, but she _____ "No." Even though she had lots of pencils.
   누군가가 그녀에게 부탁을 했지만 그녀는 "안 돼."라고 대답했다. 그녀는 많은 연필을 갖고 있었는데도 말이다.

6. My previous partner was George and I didn't _____ him, either.
   내 이전의 짝은 조지였고 나는 그 역시 좋아하지 않았다.

7. He was pretty _____.   그는 매우 거칠었다.

8. He sometimes _____ me.   그는 가끔 나를 놀렸다.

9. He was _____ to my teacher, too.   그는 선생님께도 장난이 심했다.

10. _____ liked him, but I wanted a new partner.
    다른 사람들은 그를 좋아했지만 나는 새 짝을 원했다.

11. I want a cute and kind _____.   나는 귀엽고 상냥한 아이를 원한다.

12. Do I _____ too much?   내가 너무 불평이 많나?

New Classmates

"Bang!"

"Mom, I'm home!"

Nick shouts in an angry voice.

Mom asks Nick,

"How was your new school? How were your new c_____?"

"They are a_____! My partner Justin is very s_____.

He said no when I asked to _____ a pencil.

Matthew is n_____. I gave the wrong _____ in class.

Then, he _____ me by saying, 'Don't you know the answer?'

He did that in front of everyone. Grace c_____ over and over.

Mom, I really don't _____ this school. I want to go back to my
old school."

Mom says, "I'm sure there is a good _____."

At that moment, Nick remembers a girl.

"Ah, a girl named Michelle was different from the _____.

She was kind. And her smile was lovely."

Mom says happily, "It's always _____ on the first day.

Everything will be all right. Cheer up, son."

Word Box

tough   kid   borrow   complains   classmates   teased

answer   naughty   others   awful   like   selfish

Unit 2
A Swimming Race

A Freestyle Swimming Race

★ 초등 기본어휘 ◐ 중등 기본어휘 ▲ 확장어휘

1
★ **that**
졉 ~라는 것
때 저것 혱 저
that

2
★ **second**
몡 초
혱 두 번째의
second

3
★ **take place**
굿 개최되다
윤 be held 개최되다
take place

4
★ **do one's best**
굿 최선을 다하다
do one's best

5
★ **catch up with**
굿 따라잡다
catch up with

6
★ **neck and neck**
굿 막상막하로, 비등하게

neck and neck

7
◐ **block**
몡 블록, 구역
윤 zone 구역
block

8
◐ **record**
몡 기록
됭 기록하다
record

9
◐ **result**
몡 결과, 결실
윤 outcome 결과
result

10
◐ **signal**
몡 신호
됭 신호를 보내다
윤 sign 기호, 신호
signal

11
◐ **predict**
됭 예측하다
윤 forecast 예측하다
predict

12
◐ **powerfully**
븟 힘차게, 강력하게
혱 powerful 강력한
몡 power 힘
powerfully

A 주어진 철자를 바르게 배열하여 빈칸에 알맞은 단어를 쓰세요.

1. seturl   →   a test _____ 시험 결과
2. lanisg   →   a traffic _____ 교통 신호
3. stbe   →   Do your _____. 최선을 다해라.
4. kecn nad knec   →   _____ _____ _____ in the race
   경주에서 막상막하로
5. droecr   →   the world _____ 세계 기록
6. cieprdt   →   _____ the weather 날씨를 예측하다
7. saetk laepc   →   A soccer game _____ _____.
   축구 경기가 개최된다.
8. hatt   →   I think _____ it will be rainy. 내 생각에 비가 올 것 같다.
9. dncseo   →   1 minute 25 _____s 1분 25초
10. okblc   →   three _____s 세 구역
11. feyuwporll   →   push _____ 힘차게 밀다
12. achct pu wthi   →   _____ _____ _____ him 그를 따라잡다

B 연관되는 단어를 알아보고, 빈칸에 영어 또는 우리말 뜻을 쓰세요.

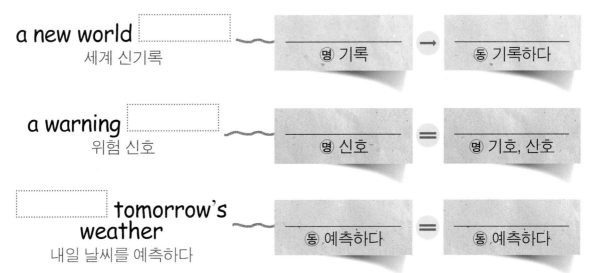

a new world [_____]
세계 신기록
_____ 명 기록 → _____ 동 기록하다

a warning [_____]
위험 신호
_____ 명 신호 = _____ 명 기호, 신호

[_____] tomorrow's weather
내일 날씨를 예측하다
_____ 동 예측하다 = _____ 동 예측하다

C 빈칸에 알맞은 단어를 쓰고, 사다리를 타고 내려가 정답을 확인하세요.

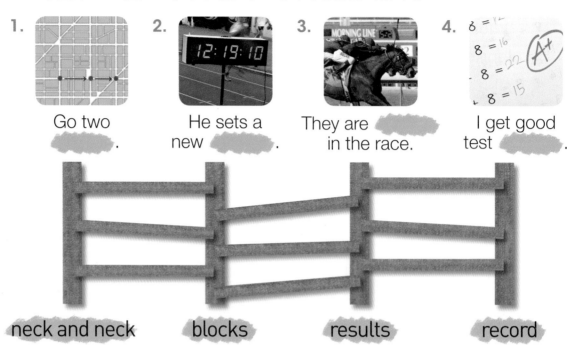

1. Go two _____.
2. He sets a new _____.
3. They are _____ in the race.
4. I get good test _____.

neck and neck   blocks   results   record

D 문장을 읽고, 빈칸에 알맞은 단어를 쓰세요.

1. The 2008 Olympic Games _____ _____ in China.
   2008년 올림픽 경기가 중국에서 열렸다.

2. Everyone _____ _____ _____ for their country.
   모두가 자기 나라를 위해 최선을 다했다.

3. Many people hoped _____ their country would win the games.
   많은 사람들이 자기 나라가 경기들에서 이기기를 바랐다.

4. But they could not _____ the result of the games.
   하지만 그들은 경기 결과를 예측할 수 없었다.

5. Eight runners started running when they got the _____ in the 100 meter final.   8명의 달리기 선수가 100미터 결승전 신호가 나자 달리기 시작했다.

6. Richard Thompson tried to _____ _____ _____ Usain Bolt.   리차드 톰슨이 우사인 볼트를 따라잡으려고 시도했다.

7. Bolt ran _____ to win the race. He ran the 100 m in 9.58 _____.
   볼트는 경주에서 이기기 위해 힘차게 달렸다. 그는 100미터를 9.58초에 달렸다.

A Freestyle Swimming* Race

A 400 m freestyle swimming race is _____ _____ now.

Five swimmers are at the starting _____.

We expect _____ it will be a close race.

The swimmers are waiting for the starting _____.

"Bang!" They dive into the pool.

They are swimming _____.

Andrew turns first.

Mike and Robin turn after him.

Eric turns last.

All five swimmers _____.

They are swimming _____ _____ _____.

We cannot p_____ the r_____ of this race.

Oh! Eric _____ _____ _____ the other swimmers.

What a surprise! Eric is in the lead*.

He touches the wall first. He is the winner.

He finishes in 3 minutes 58 _____.

It's a new _____. It was an exciting race.

*freestyle swimming 자유형 수영 be in the lead 선두에 있다

Word Box

| taking place | do their best | signal | neck and neck | blocks | seconds |
| powerfully | predict | record | results | catches up with | that |

• Lesson 2 • Turtle, the Lifesaver

✪ 초등 기본어휘　◯ 중등 기본어휘　⬠ 확장어휘

1
✪ **left**
형 왼쪽의　명 왼쪽
반 right 오른쪽의; 오른쪽
동 떠났다(leave의 과거형)

left

2
✪ **than**
접 전 ~보다

than

3
✪ **go back**
구 되돌아가다
유 return 되돌아가다

go back

4
✪ **run away**
구 달아나다
유 escape 달아나다

run away

5
◯ **save**
동 구하다, 저장하다
명 saver 구원자

save

6
◯ **toward**
전 ~쪽으로, ~을 향해

toward

7
◯ **anymore**
부 더 이상
(부정문과 함께 쓰임)

anymore

8
◯ **lifesaver**
명 생명의 은인, 인명 구조자

lifesaver

9
⬠ **paddle**
동 물장구치다

paddle

10
⬠ **splash**
동 첨벙거리다

splash

11
⬠ **turtle**
명 거북이

turtle

12
⬠ **get a cramp**
구 쥐가 나다

get a cramp

A 주어진 철자를 바르게 배열하여 빈칸에 알맞은 단어를 쓰세요.

1. elifavsre → become a _____ 생명의 은인이 되다
2. eavs → _____ the Earth 지구를 구하다
3. ahtn → taller _____ her 그녀보다 키가 더 큰
4. drwato → _____ the front door 앞문을 향해
5. og abck → _____ _____ to your seat. 너의 자리로 돌아가라.
6. yanomer → I don't want it _____. 나는 더 이상 그것을 원하지 않는다.
7. rnu yawa → _____ _____ from a police officer
   경찰관으로부터 도망치다
8. lerutt → a pet _____ 애완용 거북이
9. eflt → a _____-hander 왼손잡이
10. shlaps → _____ water 물을 첨벙거리다
11. dadpel → _____ with one's feet 한 발로 물장구치다
12. egt a parcm → _____ _____ _____ in my leg
    내 다리에 쥐가 나다

B 다음 장면에 어울리는 단어나 구를 보기에서 골라 넣어 문장을 완성하세요.

than	saved	ran away	anymore

1. The zebra [_____] from the lion.

2. The lion was faster [_____] the zebra.

3. The zebra couldn't run [_____].

4. At that moment, a hunter [_____] it.

C 문장을 읽고, 빈칸에 알맞은 뜻을 쓴 후 해당하는 것을 선으로 연결하세요.

(형) 왼쪽의 •

left

(명) 왼쪽 •

Go!

(동) 떠났다 •
(leave의 과거형)

• I sit on his left.

나는 그의 _____ 에 앉는다.

• My left hand is stronger than my right hand.

내 오른쪽 손보다 _____ 손이 더 힘이 세다.

• The plane left at 12:30.

그 비행기는 12시 30분에 _____.

D 문장을 읽고, 빈칸에 알맞은 단어를 쓰세요.

1. After school, I _____ _____ home with my friends.

   방과후 나는 친구들과 함께 집에 돌아갔다.

2. I saw a _____ on the road.   나는 도로 위에 있는 거북이를 보았다.

3. The turtle's _____ leg was hurt, so it couldn't walk.

   거북이는 왼쪽 다리를 다쳐서 걸을 수가 없었다.

4. A bus was coming _____ the turtle.   버스가 거북이를 향해 오고 있었다.

5. I ran and _____ the turtle.   나는 달려가서 거북이를 구했다.

6. I was faster _____ the bus.   내가 그 버스보다 빨랐다.

7. My friends think I'm a _____ for saving the turtle.

   친구들은 내가 거북이를 구한 생명의 은인이라고 생각한다.

8. But the turtle _____ _____ from me.   하지만 거북이는 나에게서 도망갔다.

9. The next day I was _____ in the swimming pool.

   다음날 나는 수영장에서 첨벙거리고 있었다.

10. I suddenly _____ _____ _____ in my leg.

    갑자기 나는 발에 쥐가 났다.

11. So I couldn't swim _____.   그래서 나는 더 이상 수영을 할 수가 없었다.

12. At that time, the turtle appeared and taught me how to _____.

    바로 그 때, 그 거북이가 나타나 나에게 물장구치는 법을 가르쳐 주었다.

E 빈칸에 알맞은 단어를 단어 박스에서 찾아 넣어 이야기를 완성하세요.

Turtle, the Lifesaver

Nick and his friends found a _____ at the beach.

Nick tried to catch it, but the turtle _____ _____ from him.

The turtle hurried and moved quickly _____ the sea.

Nick followed it into the sea.

The turtle swam faster _____ Nick.

Justin shouted, "Nick, _____ in the water."

Grace shouted, "_____ with your hands."

Nick almost caught it.

Suddenly, he _____ _____ _____ in his foot.

He couldn't move his _____ foot.

So he couldn't swim _____ .

"Help! Help!" Nick slowly sank into the sea.

The turtle came up to Nick and carried him on his back.

The turtle took Nick to the beach.

"Turtle, thank you for _____ me. You are a _____ ."

The turtle smiled and _____ _____ into the sea.

Word Box

went back	turtle	left	ran away	got a cramp	Paddle
anymore	lifesaver	toward	saving	splash	than

Unit 3
The Tallest Building

• Lesson 1 • *Skyscraper*

☆ 초등 기본어휘　◇ 중등 기본어휘　△ 확장어휘

1
☆ **city**
명 도시
유 town 도시, 시내

city

2
☆ **tall**
형 키가 큰, 높은 반 short 키가 작은
비 taller 더 높은
최 tallest 가장 높은

tall

3
☆ **strong**
형 강한
반 weak 약한

strong

4
☆ **company**
명 회사
유 business 회사, 사업

company

5
☆ **welcome**
동 환영하다

welcome

6
◇ **steel**
명 철

steel

7
◇ **height**
명 높이, 키
형 high 높은

height

8
◇ **million**
명 백만 형 백만의
cf. thousand 천(의)

million

9
◇ **observation**
명 관찰
동 observe 관찰하다

observation

10
△ **sway**
동 흔들리다
유 shake, swing 흔들리다

sway

11
△ **skyline**
명 지평선
유 horizon 지평선, 수평선

skyline

12
△ **skyscraper**
명 고층 빌딩, 마천루

skyscraper

A 주어진 철자를 바르게 배열하여 빈칸에 알맞은 단어를 쓰세요.

1. loecewm → _____ to my house. 우리집에 온 것을 환영한다.
2. ywsa → _____ in the wind 바람에 흔들리다
3. arpksryecs → look up at the _____ 고층 건물을 올려다보다
4. lniioml → over a _____ people 백만 명이 넘는
5. togsrn → a _____ and healthy man 강하고 건강한 남자
6. iselynk → a beautiful view of the _____ 지평선의 아름다운 풍경
7. betvooiasnr → the _____ deck on the top floor 꼭대기층의 전망대
8. gthieh → seven meters in _____ 7 미터의 높이
9. etsle → strong _____ 강한 철
10. latl → a _____ tower and a tree 높은 탑과 나무
11. iyct → live in the _____ 그 도시에 살다
12. yoacpnm → work for a _____ 회사를 위해 일하다

B 연관되는 단어를 알아보고, 빈칸에 영어 또는 우리말 뜻을 쓰세요.

_____ in English 영어를 잘하는 ～ _____ 형 강한 ⟷ weak 형 _____

170 centimeters _____ 170 센티미터의 키 ～ _____ 형 키가 큰 ⟷ short 형 _____

the capital _____ 수도 ～ _____ 명 도시 = _____ 명 도시, 시내

run a _____ 회사를 운영하다 ～ _____ 명 회사 = _____ 명 회사, 사업

C 빈칸에 알맞은 단어를 쓰고, 사다리를 타고 내려가 정답을 확인하세요.

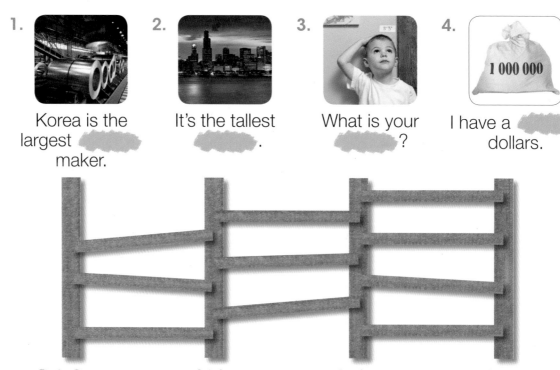

1. Korea is the largest _____ maker.

2. It's the tallest _____.

3. What is your _____?

4. I have a _____ dollars.

skyscraper   height   steel   million

D 문장을 읽고, 빈칸에 알맞은 단어를 쓰세요.

1. My dad is very _____. 나의 아빠는 키가 아주 크시다.

2. His _____ is 190 cm. 아빠 키는 190 센티미터이다.

3. He owns a _____. 그는 회사를 소유하고 계신다.

4. He runs a _____ business. 그는 강철 기업을 운영하신다.

5. The building is in the middle of the _____. 그 건물은 도시 한가운데에 있다.

6. It is one of the tallest _____. 그것은 가장 높은 고층 건물들 중 하나이다.

7. The company earns _____ of dollars a year.
   그 회사는 일 년에 수 백만 달러를 번다.

8. The _____ deck is on the 120th floor. 전망대는 120층에 있다.

 빈칸에 알맞은 단어를 단어 박스에서 찾아 넣어 이야기를 완성하세요.

Skyscraper

_____ to the Sears Tower* in Chicago.

I'm Ted, a guide for this famous s_____r.

This is one of the _____ buildings in the world.

Its _____ is about 440 meters.

It is made of _____.

It is s_____ enough to support 110 stories.

It is home to more than 100 _____.

Every year, 1.3 _____ tourists visit the Skydeck*.

Let's take the elevator and go up to the Skydeck.

It only takes 60 seconds to get to the top.

Here is the o_____ deck.

The Skydeck is on the 103rd floor.

Can you feel how the building _____ on this windy day?

Can you see far over the _____ and across Lake Michigan?

Look outside. The Chicago _____ is so wonderful.

*Sears Tower 미국의 시카고에 있는 고층 건물로 Willis Tower라고도 함
 Skydeck Sears Tower의 103층에 있는 전망대 이름

Word Box

sways   steel   tallest   height   skyline   Welcome

companies   million   strong   skyscraper   observation   city

☆ 초등 기본어휘 ◇ 중등 기본어휘 ⬠ 확장어휘

1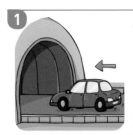

☆ **into**
전 ~ 안으로, ~ 속으로
반 out of ~ 밖으로
구 be into ~을 좋아하다

into

2

☆ **floor**
명 마루, 층
유 story 층

floor

3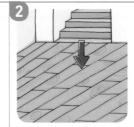

☆ **stone**
명 돌
유 rock 암석

stone

4

☆ **quickly**
부 빨리
반 slowly 천천히

quickly

5

◇ **dust**
명 먼지
형 dusty 먼지가 낀

dust

6

◇ **brick**
명 벽돌

brick

7

◇ **order**
동 명령하다, 주문하다
명 명령, 순서, 질서, 주문
유 command 명령하다

order

8

◇ **storm**
명 폭풍(우) 파 thunderstorm
뇌우, snowstorm 눈보라,
windstorm 폭풍

storm

9

◇ **heaven**
명 하늘, 천국
반 hell 지옥

heaven

10

◇ **destroy**
동 파괴하다, 멸망하다
명 destruction 파괴
반 build, construct 건설하다

destroy

11

◇ **collapse**
동 (건물 등이) 무너지다
유 crumble 무너지다

collapse

12

⬠ **tornado**
명 토네이도, (강력한) 폭풍

tornado

A 주어진 철자를 바르게 배열하여 빈칸에 알맞은 단어를 쓰세요.

1. sdetryo → _____ the building with a bomb 폭탄으로 빌딩을 파괴하다
2. rreod → give an _____ 명령을 내리다
3. rloof → the first _____ 1층
4. rtsmo → a terrible _____ 심한 폭풍우
5. rtndooa → a _____ in the desert 사막에서의 토네이도
6. etsno → a building made of _____ 돌로 만들어진 건물
7. salopcel → _____ under the weight of the books 책의 무게로 무너지다
8. tnio → rush _____ the kitchen 부엌으로 뛰어 들어오다
9. tdus → yellow _____ 황사
10. rcbki → lay _____s 벽돌을 쌓다
11. eehvna → _____ on earth 지상 낙원
12. luyqkic → go out _____ 빨리 나가다

B 다음 장면에 어울리는 단어를 보기에서 골라 넣어 문장을 완성하세요.

| storm | collapse | tornado | quickly |

1. A _____ is blowing through the city.
2. A terrible _____ starts.
3. A building is about to _____.
4. People should move _____.

C 문장을 읽고, 빈칸에 알맞은 뜻을 쓴 후 해당하는 것을 선으로 연결하세요.

명 순서, 차례 ●   ● Put the names in <u>order</u>.
                         이름들을 _____대로 놓으세요.

명 질서 ●   ● I <u>ordered</u> her to go out.
                         나는 그녀에게 나가라고 _____.

order

명 명령 ●   ● Preserve law and <u>order</u>.
동 명령하다   법과 _____를 지켜라.

Go!

명 주문 ●   ● May I take your <u>order</u>?
동 주문하다   _____ 하시겠습니까?

D 문장을 읽고, 빈칸에 알맞은 단어를 쓰세요.

1. Josh studies on the 2nd _____ at school.   조쉬는 학교 2층에서 공부한다.

2. He sees a _____ out the window.
   그는 창문 밖으로 회오리 바람을 본다.

3. The red _____ from the wall fall down. Many _____ are also flying.   벽의 빨간 벽돌들이 떨어져 나간다. 많은 돌들도 날아다닌다.

4. The teacher comes _____ the classroom.   선생님이 교실 안으로 들어오신다.

5. He _____ the students to move.   그는 학생들에게 이동하라고 명령하신다.

6. "Go to the basement _____."   "빨리 지하실로 가거라."

7. The hallway is full of _____.   복도는 먼지로 가득하다.

8. Our school suddenly _____.   학교가 갑자기 무너진다.

9. After the _____, it's very calm.   폭풍우 뒤에 아주 고요하다.

10. It _____ed our school. _____ will help us.
    그것이 우리 학교를 파괴했다. 하늘이 우리를 도울 것이다.

 빈칸에 알맞은 단어를 단어 박스에서 찾아 넣어 이야기를 완성하세요.

The Tower of Babel

One day, Nick sees a picture of a tall tower.

A t_____ suddenly appears.

It takes him _____ the picture.

Some people are making b_____ out of straw.

A director gives an _____ to Nick.

"Carry the bricks to the tower."

An old man says,

"Come on. Just drag them _____."

The king shouts, "We will build the Tower of Babel.

The tower will go high up into h_____."

Nick says, "Oh, no. You need strong _____ and wood

to support it."

Soon, a _____ is blowing angrily.

The tower _____ in a cloud of smoke.

People scream and are covered in _____.

Nick drops down on the _____ from the picture.

Now, the Tower of Babel is d_____.

Word Box

floor   heaven   collapses   order   quickly   stones

destroyed   into   tornado   dust   storm   bricks

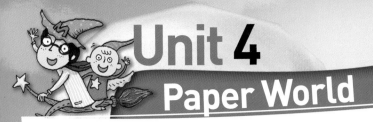

Unit 4
Paper World

✪ 초등 기본어휘 ◇ 중등 기본어휘 ⬡ 확장어휘

1 ✪ **no**
형 하나도 없는, ~도 없는
부 아니

no

2 ✪ **ago**
부 전에
유 before 전에

ago

3 ✪ **then**
부 그 때에, 그 다음에

then

4 ✪ **wetland**
명 (보통 복수형) 습지대

wetland

5 ✪ **sunlight**
명 햇빛
유 sunshine 햇빛

sunlight

6 ◇ **part**
명 부분
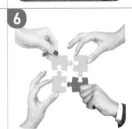

part

7 ◇ **sheet**
명 (종이) 한 장, 시트

sheet

8 ◇ **strip**
명 가늘고 긴 조각
동 (껍질 등을) 벗기다

strip

9 ◇ **origin**
명 기원, 유래
형 original 최초의, 기원의

origin

10 ◇ **ancient**
형 고대의
반 modern 현대의

ancient

11 ◇ **century**
명 세기, 100년

century

12 ⬡ **soak**
동 적시다, 담그다

soak

 A 주어진 철자를 바르게 배열하여 빈칸에 알맞은 단어를 쓰세요.

1. ewltnad → live in the _____s 습지에 살다
2. aptr → an important _____ of the book 그 책의 중요한 부분
3. norgii → the _____ of mankind 인류의 기원
4. esteh → a _____ of paper 종이 한 장
5. trpis → use a _____ of paper 가느다란 종이 조각을 이용하다
6. oga → I went to Disneyland a long time _____.
   나는 오래 전에 디즈니랜드에 갔었다.
7. tneicna → the _____ Romans 고대 로마인들
8. on → _____ man is without his faults. 결점이 없는 사람은 없다.
9. stnglihu → the bright morning _____ 밝은 아침 햇빛
10. asko → _____ in hot water 뜨거운 물에 담그다
11. yrutcne → the twenty-first _____ 21세기
12. ehnt → every now and _____ 가끔씩

B 연관되는 단어를 알아보고, 빈칸에 영어 또는 우리말 뜻을 쓰세요.

five years [_____]
5년 전에

_____ 부 전에 = _____ 부 전에

the strong [_____]
강한 햇빛

_____ 명 햇빛 = _____ 명 햇빛

the [_____] of life
생명의 기원

_____ 명 기원, 유래 → _____ 형 최초의, 기원의

an [_____] city
고대 도시

_____ 형 고대의 ↔ _____ 형 현대의

C 빈칸에 알맞은 단어를 쓰고, 사다리를 타고 내려가 정답을 확인하세요.

1. _____ are very important for wildlife.

2. There are _____ plants in the desert.

3. We live in the 21st _____.

4. _____ the rice in water.

Wetlands　　Soak　　century　　no

D 문장을 읽고, 빈칸에 알맞은 단어를 쓰세요.

1. Long _____, what did people write on?　오래 전에 사람들은 어디에 글씨를 썼을까?

2. The _____ of paper is Papyrus.　종이의 기원은 파피루스이다.

3. The Egyptians cut the papyrus plant into _____.
   이집트인들은 식물 파피루스를 가느다란 조각들로 잘랐다.

4. They put them in the _____ to dry.
   그들은 그것들을 말리기 위해 햇빛 아래에 놓아두었다.

5. They linked _____ of papyrus and made a roll.
   그들은 파피루스의 부분들을 연결하여 롤을 만들었다.

6. The _____ people used parchment, too.　고대인들은 양피지도 사용했다.

7. And _____, paper was invented in China.
   그리고 나서, 종이가 중국에서 발명되었다.

8. A _____ of paper is thin and light.　종이 한 장은 얇고 가볍다.

 빈칸에 알맞은 단어를 단어 박스에서 찾아 넣어 이야기를 완성하세요.

Papyrus*

Papyrus is a plant which grows in w_____.

It is also the world's first paper.

It was used by the _____ Egyptians*.

Can you imagine if there was _____ paper in the world?

We can't imagine a world without paper.

How did the Egyptians make paper thousands of years _____?

They peeled off the outer _____ of the papyrus plant.

They cut the inner part into thin st_____.

Next, they _____ the papyrus plant strips in water.

_____, what do you think happened?

They flattened* the strips into sh_____.

Lastly, the sheets were dried in the _____.

The _____ of the word "paper" comes from "papyrus."

Papyrus was used until the 8th _____.

*papyrus 파피루스 Egyptian 이집트인 flatten 평평하게 펴다

Word Box

ago   wetlands   strips   sunlight   no   Then

sheets   part   ancient   soaked   origin   century

Magic Drawing Paper

☆ 초등 기본어휘 ◇ 중등 기본어휘 △ 확장어휘

1

☆ **erase**
동 지우다
명 eraser 지우개

erase

2

☆ **listen**
동 듣다
유 hear 듣다

listen

3

☆ **sketch**
명 스케치
동 스케치하다

sketch

4

☆ **art class**
명 미술 수업

art class

5

☆ **drawing paper**
명 도화지

drawing paper

6

☆ **look around**
구 좌우를 둘러보다

look around

7

☆ **give out light**
구 빛을 내다

give out light

8

◇ **rub**
동 문지르다, 비비다

rub

9

◇ **wave**
동 흔들다 명 파도, 파장
유 shake, swing 흔들다
형 wavy 곱슬거리는

wave

10

◇ **realize**
동 깨닫다

realize

11

◇ **everything**
대 모든 것

everything

12

△ **pop out**
구 튀어나오다

pop out

A 주어진 철자를 바르게 배열하여 빈칸에 알맞은 단어를 쓰세요.

1. opp uot → _____ _____ at the box 상자에서 튀어나오다
2. vaew → _____ their hands 그들의 손을 흔들다
3. bur → _____ my eyes 나의 눈을 비비다
4. atr slasc → have _____ _____ on Monday
   월요일에 미술 수업이 있다
5. okol oudnar → _____ _____ you 네 주위를 둘러보다
6. seaer → _____ his memory 그의 기억을 지우다
7. nrawgdi ppare → a pencil on the _____ _____
   도화지 위의 연필 한 자루
8. elstni → _____ to your mother. 어머니 말씀을 들으렴.
9. teegnihvry → _____ about board games 보드 게임에 관한 모든 것
10. leaeizr → _____ how expensive it is
    그것이 얼마나 비싼지 깨닫다
11. schtek → make a _____ of a cat 고양이를 스케치하다
12. giev uot ihgtl → A lamp _____s _____ _____.
    램프가 빛을 낸다.

B 다음 장면에 어울리는 단어를 보기에서 골라 넣어 문장을 완성하세요.

listening   art class   drawing paper   sketch

1. The girls have [_____].
2. The little girl is [_____] to her teacher.
3. The teacher is teaching how to [_____].
4. The older girl is painting on [_____].

C 문장을 읽고, 빈칸에 알맞은 뜻을 쓴 후 해당하는 것을 선으로 연결하세요.

(명) 파도 •

(명) 파장 •

wave

Go!

(동) 흔들다 •

(형) 곱슬거리는 •

wavy

• My mom <u>waved</u> her hands at me.
  엄마는 나에게 손을 _____.

• A <u>wave</u> of fear spread.
  두려움의 _____이 퍼졌다.

• He rides the <u>waves</u> at the beach.
  그는 해변에서 _____를 탄다.

• His hair is <u>wavy</u>.
  그의 머리는 _____.

D 문장을 읽고, 빈칸에 알맞은 단어를 쓰세요.

1. I have _____ _____ today. 나는 오늘 미술 수업이 있다.

2. The topic is _____ with your eyes closed.
   주제는 눈감고 스케치하기이다.

3. I can't _____ my drawing. 나는 내 그림을 지울 수 없다.

4. But I can _____ the paper. 그러나 나는 종이를 문지를 수는 있다.

5. I start to draw on the _____ _____. 나는 도화지 위에 그림을 그리기 시작한다.

6. Suddenly, _____ goes dark. 갑자기 모든 것이 어두워진다.

7. I _____ _____. 나는 주위를 둘러본다.

8. I _____ my hands but nobody is there. 나는 손을 흔들지만 아무도 없다.

9. I hear a voice, "Is anybody there? _____ to me."
   나는 어떤 목소리를 듣는다. "거기 누구 없어요? 제 말 좀 들어보세요."

10. Something outside _____ _____ _____.
    밖에서 무언가가 빛을 낸다.

11. It _____ _____ from behind the door. 그것은 문 뒤에서 튀어나온다.

12. I _____ that it's a dream. 나는 그것이 꿈이라는 것을 깨닫는다.

Magic Drawing Paper

Nick has _____ _____ outdoors.

Today's activity is to draw the area around his school.

Nick is s_____ trees and rides* in the playground.

He e_____ parts of a tall tree.

So, the tree _____ _____ _____.

Then, he falls on a white floor.

_____ around him is white.

When he sees the tall tree,

he _____ that he is in the paper.

He wants to get out of the

_____ _____.

Nick climbs up the tall tree and _____ _____.

"Is anybody here? _____ to me!"

Nick shouts and _____ his hands.

Nick's friends Justin and Michelle are looking for him.

They hear Nick's voice and find him in the drawing paper.

Justin draws a door and r_____ the paper.

Then, the door opens, and poor Nick _____ _____

of the paper.

*ride 타는 놀이기구, 타기

Word Box

looks around | sketching | drawing paper | erases | Listen | realizes

pops out | art class | gives out light | waves | Everything | rubs

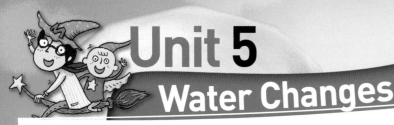

Unit 5
Water Changes

• Lesson 1 • *The Water Cycle*

☆ 초등 기본어휘 ◇ 중등 기본어휘 △ 확장어휘

1
☆ **or**
졉 또는, 혹은

or

2
☆ **up**
뷔 위로

up

3

☆ **down**
뷔 아래로

down

4

☆ **river**
멩 (큰) 강
윤 stream 작은 강

river

5

◇ **heat**
멩 열 똥 뜨겁게 하다
권 heat up 점점 뜨거워지다,
   활기를 띠다

heat

6
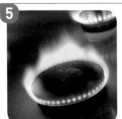
◇ **flow**
똥 흐르다

flow

7

◇ **form**
멩 모습, 형태
똥 형성하다
윤 figure 모습

form

8
◇ **rise**
똥 일어서다, 올라가다
반 fall 떨어지다

rise

9

◇ **surface**
멩 표면, 평면

surface

10

△ **water drop**
멩 물방울

water drop

11

△ **water cycle**
멩 물의 순환

water cycle

12

△ **water vapor**
멩 수증기

water vapor

A 주어진 철자를 바르게 배열하여 빈칸에 알맞은 단어를 쓰세요.

1. ro ➔ to be _____ not to be 사느냐 죽느냐
2. omrf ➔ basic _____ 기본 형태
3. pu ➔ look _____ 위를 보다
4. eisr ➔ _____ high 높이 올라가다
5. donw ➔ jump _____ 아래로 뛰어내리다
6. tewar dpro ➔ a picture of a _____ _____ 물방울 사진
7. iverr ➔ the Han _____ 한강
8. awter ccyle ➔ Earth's _____ _____ 지구의 물의 순환
9. haet ➔ _____ system 난방 시설
10. retaw vropa ➔ hot _____ _____ 뜨거운 수증기
11. flwo ➔ _____ over 흘러넘치다
12. usracef ➔ _____ temperature 표면 온도

B 연관되는 단어를 알아보고, 빈칸에 영어 또는 우리말 뜻을 쓰세요.

Hands ☐☐☐☐☐ !
손들어!

_____ ↔ _____
(부) 위로   (부) 아래로

a bridge across the ☐☐☐☐☐
강을 가로지르는 다리

_____ = _____
(명) (큰) 강   (명) 작은 강

The ☐☐☐☐☐ has changed.
형태가 바뀌었다.

_____ = _____
(명) 모습, 형태   (명) 모습

C 빈칸에 알맞은 단어를 쓰고, 사다리를 타고 내려가 정답을 확인하세요.

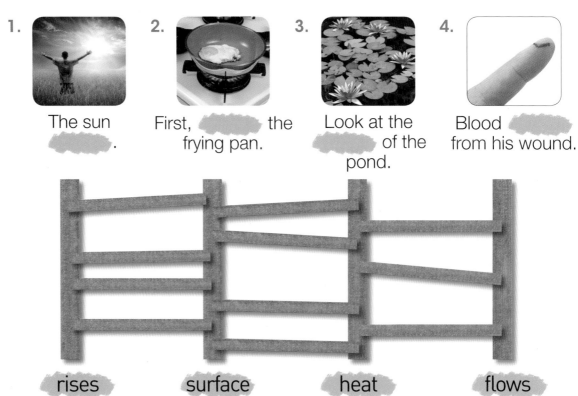

1. The sun _____.

2. First, _____ the frying pan.

3. Look at the _____ of the pond.

4. Blood _____ from his wound.

rises   surface   heat   flows

D 문장을 읽고, 빈칸에 알맞은 단어를 쓰세요.

1. Is water from the sky _____ the oceans? 물은 하늘에서 오나 또는 바다에서 오나?

2. Let's learn about the _____ _____. 물의 순환에 대해 배워보자.

3. Let's _____ a group to study about water.
   물에 대해 공부하기 위해 그룹을 구성하자.

4. What happens? Look _____ there. 무슨 일이지? 저 위를 봐.

5. _____ _____ goes up into the sky. 수증기가 하늘로 올라간다.

6. It goes up from a _____. 이것은 강에서부터 올라간다.

7. We can see a _____ _____ as rain. 우리는 비로 물방울을 볼 수 있다.

8. It comes _____ from the sky. 이것은 하늘로부터 아래로 온다.

 빈칸에 알맞은 단어를 단어 박스에서 찾아 넣어 이야기를 완성하세요.

The Water Cycle

70% of the Earth's _____ is water.

The sun shines on the _____.

It h_____ the water.

Water becomes w_____ v_____.

Water vapor _____ from the river.

It goes _____ into the sky.

Water vapor gets cold and becomes _____ _____.

Water drops come together and _____ clouds.

Water drops in the clouds come back to earth.

They fall into the rivers as rain _____ snow.

Water flows _____ from upper streams.*

The rivers _____ into the oceans.

And the _____ _____ begins again.

*upper stream 상류

Word Box

down   heats   flow   or   water drops   rises

water vapor   water cycle   up   river   surface   form

A Wonderful Experience

✪ 초등 기본어휘 ◇ 중등 기본어휘 ⬡ 확장어휘

1

✪ **cool**
- (형) 멋진, 시원한
- (반) hot 더운

cool

2

✪ **cover**
- (명) 뚜껑, 표지, 덮개
- (동) 덮다, 감추다, 포함하다 (구) be covered with ~으로 뒤덮이다

cover

3

✪ **sheep**
- (명) 양

sheep

4

✪ **person**
- (명) 사람
- (복) people 사람들
- (구) in person 자신이 직접

person

5

◇ **ocean**
- (명) 바다

ocean

6

◇ **a lot of**
- (구) 많은
- (유) lots of 많은

a lot of

7
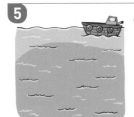

◇ **freeze**
- (동) 얼게 하다, 움직이지 않다
- (형) frozen 추워서 꽁꽁 얼 것 같은

freeze

8

◇ **lighten**
- (동) 가벼워지다, 가볍게 해주다
- (구) lighten up 기운내다

lighten

9

◇ **turn into**
- (구) 변하다

turn into

10

⬡ **chilly**
- (형) 차가운, 냉담한, 추운

chilly

11

⬡ **evaporate**
- (동) 증발하다, 사라지다
- (유) dry 마르다
- (명) evaporation 증발

evaporate

12

⬡ **each other**
- (구) 서로

each other

A 주어진 철자를 바르게 배열하여 빈칸에 알맞은 단어를 쓰세요.

1. revco → a piano _____ 피아노 덮개
2. trnu toin → _____ _____ ashes 재로 변하다
3. tol fo → a _____ _____ homework 많은 숙제
4. eapaterov → the water _____s 물이 증발한다
5. oolc → _____ weather 시원한 날씨
6. hillcy → _____ wind 차가운 바람
7. eeerfz → _____ over 얼어붙다
8. aceh thoer → We know _____ _____. 우리는 서로 안다.
9. aceno → Pacific _____ 태평양
10. ighltne → _____ up! 기운내라!
11. rsonep → in _____ 자신이 직접
12. eesph → a _____ on the hill 언덕 위의 양 한 마리

B 다음 장면에 어울리는 단어나 구를 보기에서 골라 넣어 문장을 완성하세요.

a lot of	covered	sheep	lightens

1. Mom, look at _____.

2. Yes, they are _____ in wool.

3. People need to shear* the sheep to get _____ wool.

4. It _____ the sheep.

*shear (양의) 털을 깎다

C 문장을 읽고, 빈칸에 알맞은 뜻을 쓴 후 해당하는 것을 선으로 연결하세요.

cover   Go!

명 표지, 덮개 •

동 덮다, 씌우다 •

동 감추다, 숨기다•

동 포함하다 •

• The papers cover the table.
그 종이들이 책상을 _____.

• Don't judge a book by its cover.
_____ 만 보고 책을 판단하지 말라.

• The book covers five stories.
그 책은 다섯 개의 이야기를 _____.

• He covers the truth.
그는 진실을 _____.

D 문장을 읽고, 빈칸에 알맞은 단어를 쓰세요.

1. He goes up the hill with _____ _____ _____ friends.
그는 많은 친구들과 언덕 위로 간다.

2. The _____ wind blows.   시원한 바람이 불어온다.

3. He feels gloomy but the wind _____ his mood.
그는 우울하지만 바람이 그의 기분을 가볍게 해준다.

4. When he feels better, he _____ _____ a sheep.
그가 기분이 좋아졌을 때 그는 양으로 변한다.

5. He is _____ in wool.   그는 양털로 덮여있다.

6. His friends see the _____.   그의 친구들이 그 양을 본다.

7. They look at _____ _____.   그들은 서로 쳐다본다.

8. Suddenly, they feel _____.   갑자기 그들은 추위를 느낀다.

9. They feel _____ like ice.   그들은 얼음처럼 꽁꽁 얼어붙은 느낌이 든다.

10. A _____ comes to him and whispers.   한 사람이 그에게 와서 속삭인다.

11. "Your friends will _____ like water soon."
"네 친구들은 곧 물처럼 증발할 거야."

12. "You can meet them in the _____."   "너는 그들을 바다에서 만날 수 있어."

A Wonderful Experience

It is a cloudy day.

The sky is _____ with clouds.

The clouds look like a flock of s_____.

Nick closes his eyes and lies

on a tube in the _____.

Nick feels his body l_____.

When he opens his eyes,

he _____ _____ water.

He e_____ and goes up into the sky.

He has _____ _____ _____ friends in the sky.

It is very ch_____ in the sky.

Nick and his friends hug _____ _____.

They f_____ and become snow.

They feel heavy, so they fall down into the ocean.

At that moment, Nick turns into a _____ again.

"Wow! That was so _____!

It was such a wonderful experience."

Word Box

| sheep | person | ocean | each other | freeze | chilly |
| a lot of | covered | evaporates | cool | turns into | lighten |

Unit 6
About Junk Food

☆ 초등 기본어휘 ◇ 중등 기본어휘 ⬢ 확장어휘

1
☆ **as**
전 ~ 같이, ~처럼
접 ~하는 동안에, ~ 때문에
구 as follows 다음과 같이

as

2
☆ **test**
동 시험하다, 검사하다 명 시험
유 exam 시험 구 test the
waters 미리 상황을 살피다

test

3
☆ **movie**
명 영화
유 film 영화

movie

4
☆ **weight**
명 체중, 무게
동 weigh 무게가 ~이다

weight

5
☆ **throw up**
구 토하다
유 vomit 토하다

throw up

6
◇ **meal**
명 식사

meal

7
◇ **limit**
동 제한하다
명 제한
유 limitation 제한

limit

8
◇ **offer**
동 제안하다, 제공하다
유 suggest 제안하다

offer

9
◇ **distance**
명 거리
형 distant 거리가 먼

distance

10
◇ **depression**
명 우울증
동 depress 우울하게 만들다
형 depressed 우울한

depression

11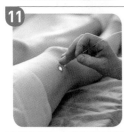
◇ **treatment**
명 치료
동 treat 치료하다

treatment

12
⬢ **quit**
동 그만두다
유 stop 멈추다
give up 포기하다

quit

 주어진 철자를 바르게 배열하여 빈칸에 알맞은 단어를 쓰세요.

1. vemio → see a _____ 영화를 보다
2. lema → a delicious_____ 맛있는 식사
3. ferof → _____ me a job 나에게 일자리를 제안하다
4. tiqu → _____ a job 일을 그만두다
5. rtetmneta → first-aid _____ 응급 처치
6. sa → _____ follows 다음과 같이
7. timil → the speed _____ 속도 제한
8. dscienta → keep your _____ 거리를 유지하다
9. hteigw → lose _____ 살이 빠지다
10. etts → _____ the waters 미리 상황을 살피다, 의중을 떠보다
11. wtrho pu → want to _____ _____ 토하고 싶다
12. dneopirses → mental _____ 우울증

 연관되는 단어를 알아보고, 빈칸에 영어 또는 우리말 뜻을 쓰세요.

show a _____ ~~~~ _____ = _____
영화를 상영하다   명 영화   명 영화

_____ a preference ~~~~ _____ = _____
우선권을 제공하다   동 제공하다, 제안하다   동 제안하다

_____ your memory ~~~~ _____ → _____
당신의 기억력을 시험하다   동 시험하다, 검사하다   명 시험

_____ my job ~~~~ _____ = give up
나의 일을 그만두다   동 그만두다   구 _____

C 빈칸에 알맞은 단어를 쓰고, 사다리를 타고 내려가 정답을 확인하세요.

1. I want to ___ weight.

2. He ___ his help to her.

3. What can I eat for a light ___?

4. This movie has an age ___ of 12 and over.

offers   limit   lose   meal

D 문장을 읽고, 빈칸에 알맞은 단어를 쓰세요.

1. I went to see a 3D _____ . 나는 3D 영화를 보러 갔다.

2. I felt like it was real _____ I watched the movie.
   나는 그 영화를 보는 동안에 실제 있는 일처럼 느껴졌다.

3. I felt that everything in the movie was not in _____ .
   나는 그 영화에 나오는 모든 것들이 멀리 있다고 느껴지지 않았다.

4. But I had to _____ watching the movie.
   그러나 나는 그 영화를 보는 것을 그만둬야 했다.

5. Because I felt like _____ _____ . 왜냐하면 나는 토할 것 같았기 때문이다.

6. I saw a doctor and he ran some _____ . 나는 의사에게 갔고 그는 몇가지 검사들을 했다.

7. I got some _____ and felt better. 나는 치료를 받았고 좋아졌다.

8. But I felt _____ because I couldn't finish the movie.
   그렇지만 영화를 다 볼 수 없어서 나는 우울했다.

Fast Food

Morgan Spurlock made the _____ *Super Size Me*.
He _____ the bad effects of fast food on himself.
He carried out a program _____ follows.

1. He ate three _____ a day
    at a fast-food restaurant for thirty days.

2. If a restaurant worker _____ to
    supersize the meal, he accepted the offer.

3. He _____ himself to walking 1~2 km a day.
    That is the average _____ Americans walk daily.

He got _____ from a doctor regularly during his program.
He _____ _____ after eating fast food 4 days later.
His _____ increased from 85 kg to 96 kg in a month.
He also got symptoms of d_____ and high blood pressure*.
To be healthy again, he had to _____ eating fast food.

＊**high blood pressure** 고혈압

Word Box

offered	treatment	as	tested	depression	meals
weight	movie	limited	distance	threw up	quit

• Lesson 2 • Burger Fighting

1
✪ **hate**
동 몹시 싫어하다
명 증오
유 dislike 싫어하다

hate

2
✪ **fresh**
형 신선한

fresh

3
✪ **today**
부 오늘

today

4
✪ **woman**
명 여자 유 lady 여자, 여성
반 man 남자
복 women 여자들

woman

5
✪ **way**
명 길, 방식, 방향 부 훨씬
구 on the way home
집에 가는 길에

way

6
✪ **fall under a spell**
구 마법에 걸리다
유 be under a spell
마법에 걸리다

fall under a spell

7
◯ **human**
명 사람, 인간
유 person 사람

human

8
◯ **regret**
동 후회하다

regret

9
◯ **remove**
동 없애다, 제거하다

remove

10
◯ **already**
부 이미, 벌써

already

11
◯ **friendship**
명 우정

friendship

12
⬡ **snatch**
동 잡아채다, 낚아채다

snatch

A 주어진 철자를 바르게 배열하여 빈칸에 알맞은 단어를 쓰세요.

1. rshfe → _____ fruits 신선한 과일들
2. nuahm → _____ body 인체
3. reevmo → _____ a bad tradition 나쁜 전통을 없애다
4. omawn → career _____ 직장 여성, 커리어 우먼
5. eath → love and _____ 사랑과 증오, 애증
6. cntsah → _____ a purse 지갑을 낚아채다
7. aelayrd → sold out _____ 이미 매진된
8. ipfrdnhsei → break a _____ with ~와 우정을 끊다, 절교하다
9. gterre → _____ breaking the rules 규칙들을 어긴 것을 후회하다
10. llfe ndreu a plesl → A boy _____ _____ _____ _____. 소년이 마법에 걸렸다.
11. ayw → on the _____ home 집에 가는 길에
12. oytda → a year ago _____ 1년 전 오늘

B 다음 장면에 어울리는 단어나 구를 보기에서 골라 넣어 문장을 완성하세요.

women	on the way home	hate	regret

1. Two _____ went on a trip.
2. They are now _____.
3. They _____ spending all their money.
4. They _____ walking, so they try to hitchhike* to get home.

＊**hitchhike** 히치하이크하다, 남의 차를 얻어 타다

C 문장을 읽고, 빈칸에 알맞은 뜻을 쓴 후 해당하는 것을 선으로 연결하세요.

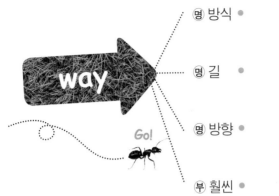

명 방식 •

명 길 •

명 방향 •

부 훨씬 •

• I want to buy a one-**way** ticket to Seoul.
나는 서울로 가는 한 _____ 티켓을 사고 싶다.

• Can you tell me the **way** to the shopping mall?
내게 쇼핑몰로 가는 _____ 을 알려줄 수 있니?

• This bag is **way** better than that one.
이 가방이 저것보다 _____ 좋다.

• I don't like the **way** she looks at me.
나는 그녀가 나를 보는 _____ 이 맘에 안 든다.

D 문장을 읽고, 빈칸에 알맞은 단어를 쓰세요.

1. Jake has a close _____ with Mike.   제이크와 마이크는 우정이 돈독하다.

2. But Mike _____ Jake's spells.   그러나 마이크는 제이크의 마법을 싫어한다.

3. He _____ Jake's magic wand.   그는 제이크의 마술봉을 잡아챈다.

4. Mike _____ _____ _____ _____ .   마이크는 마법에 걸린다.

5. Jake makes Mike smell like _____ fish.
제이크는 마이크에게서 신선한 생선 냄새가 나게 만든다.

6. But, something happened to Jake _____ .
그러나 오늘 제이크에게 무슨 일이 일어났다.

7. A _____ knows that Jake can cast spells.
어떤 여자가 제이크가 마법을 걸 수 있다는 것을 안다.

8. On the _____ home, Jake meets her.
집에 오는 길에, 제이크는 그녀를 만난다.

9. "I _____ know you cast a spell on your friend."
"난 네가 네 친구에게 마법을 거는 걸 벌써 알고 있어."

10. "To cast a spell on a _____ is not right."   "사람에게 마법을 거는 것은 옳지 않아."

11. She _____ his spell.   그녀는 그의 마법을 없앤다.

12. He _____ it but she is gone.   그는 그것을 후회하지만 그녀는 사라졌다.

Burger Fighting

Nick didn't feel well t_____.

Nick and Matthew were eating burgers on their _____ home.

Nick s_____ Matthew's burger to eat some more.

"You're so bad. I _____ you!" shouted Matthew.

An old _____ dropped her fruit basket in front of them.

Nick picked up the fruit and gave it to her.

She thanked Nick and gave him some _____ fruit.

When he ate a peach, his body changed into a burger.

He found Matthew, but Matthew had a_____ become a burger.

Nick and Matthew _____ _____ _____ _____
because of their fight.

When they _____ fighting, the old woman appeared.

She made sure that their _____ was still strong.

So she _____ the spell.

They changed back into _____ again.

They promised not to fight anymore.

Word Box

woman | regretted | way | fresh | removed | hate

snatched | already | friendship | fell under a spell | today | humans

Unit 7
The Seven Stars

• Lesson 1 • *The Big Dipper*

1
☆ **once**
㉑ 한 번

once

2
☆ **round**
㉐ ~을 (빙) 둘러
㉗ 둥근

round

3
☆ **almost**
㉑ 거의
㉔ nearly 거의

almost

4
◇ **bowl**
㉘ 사발

bowl

5
◇ **sailor**
㉘ 선원, 뱃사람
㉓ sail 항해하다

sailor

6
◇ **describe**
㉓ 묘사하다, 설명하다

describe

7
◇ **northern**
㉗ 북쪽의
㉘ north 북쪽

northern

8
◇ **position**
㉘ 위치
㉔ location 위치

position

9
◇ **direction**
㉘ 방향, 지시
㉓ direct 지시하다
㉗ direct 똑바른, 직접의

direction

10
△ **ox**
㉘ 황소
㉫ oxen 황소들
㉑ cow 암소

ox

11
△ **wagon**
㉘ 마차, 수레

wagon

12
△ **constellation**
㉘ 별자리

constellation

A 주어진 철자를 바르게 배열하여 빈칸에 알맞은 단어를 쓰세요.

1. neoc → _____ a week   일주일에 한 번
2. oblw → a salad _____   샐러드 그릇
3. tlaoms → _____ fell off   거의 떨어질 뻔한
4. awogn → a horse-drawn _____   말이 끄는 마차
5. eicodnrit → the right _____   옳은 방향
6. scetinaootlln → a _____ legend   별자리 전설
7. uordn → a _____ face   둥근 얼굴
8. xo → as strong as an _____   황소처럼 힘이 센
9. tneorrhn → Cassiopeia in the _____ sky   북쪽 하늘의 카시오페이아자리
10. rsliao → a _____ on a large ship   큰 배의 선원
11. pnsootii → hold one's _____   자신의 위치를 지키다
12. cieerbds → _____ a beautiful scene   아름다운 광경을 묘사하다

B 연관되는 단어를 알아보고, 빈칸에 영어 또는 우리말 뜻을 쓰세요.

_____ hemisphere
북반구

_____ 형 북쪽의 ➡ north
명 _____

a _____ arriving in the port
부두에 도착하는 선원

_____ 명 선원, 뱃사람 ➡ sail
동 _____

an _____ with big horns
큰 뿔을 가진 황소

_____ 명 황소 ↔ _____ 명 암소

in a good _____
유리한 위치에서

_____ 명 위치 = _____ 명 위치

C 빈칸에 알맞은 단어를 쓰고, 사다리를 타고 내려가 정답을 확인하세요.

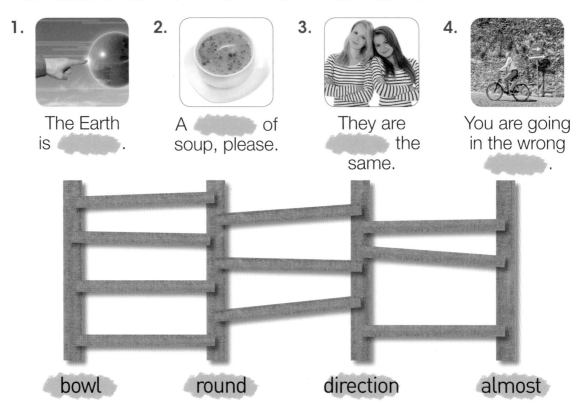

1. The Earth is _____ .

2. A _____ of soup, please.

3. They are _____ the same.

4. You are going in the wrong _____ .

bowl   round   direction   almost

D 문장을 읽고, 빈칸에 알맞은 단어를 쓰세요.

1. The _____ on deck drop the anchor.   갑판 위의 선원들이 닻을 내린다.

2. The ship has been sailing for _____ two months.
   이 배는 거의 두 달째 항해 중이다.

3. They are going to the _____ part of Africa.
   그들은 북쪽 아프리카 지역으로 가는 중이다.

4. They are carrying over 100 _____ .   그들은 100마리가 넘는 황소를 운반하고 있다.

5. They have a party _____ a week.   그들은 일주일에 한 번 파티를 한다.

6. They serve _____ full of food.   그들은 음식이 가득 든 그릇들을 차려 낸다.

7. They talk about _____ legends.   그들은 별자리 전설들에 대해서 이야기한다.

8. It is hard to _____ how beautiful the stars are.
   별들이 얼마나 아름다운지 묘사하기는 힘들다.

E 빈칸에 알맞은 단어를 단어 박스에서 찾아 넣어 이야기를 완성하세요.

The Big Dipper*

Have you ever seen stars in the sky?

Look at a group of stars in the n_____ part of the sky.

_____ everybody can find seven bright stars in a group.

They form the third largest c_____.

People call it different names, including the Big Dipper.

The ancient Greeks _____ it as a bear with a long tail.

The Romans believed that the stars looked like seven o_____.

The Vikings thought it was a w_____ traveling in the sky.

The native Americans said it looked like a _____ with a bent handle.

When ancient _____ lost their way, the Big Dipper guided them in the right d_____.

They could tell* the time by looking at the _____ of the Big Dipper.

It appears to circle _____ the North star, Polaris*, _____ a night.

*Big Dipper 북두칠성　tell 분간하다, 말하다　Polaris 북극성

Word Box

| northern | Almost | constellation | described | oxen | wagon |

| sailors | bowl | direction | position | round | once |

• Lesson 2 • Orion and the Scorpion

★ 초등 기본어휘 ◇ 중등 기본어휘 ▲ 확장어휘

1

★ **alone**
형 혼자의 부 홀로
유 lonely 외로운

alone

2

★ **never**
부 결코 ~않다
반 ever 한 번도
(not과 함께) 결코 ~않다

never

3

★ **night**
명 밤
반 day 낮

night

4

◇ **bite**
동 물다

bite

5

◇ **leave**
동 남기다, 떠나다, 맡기다
명 휴가
(과거형: left — 과거분사형: left)

leave

6

◇ **sword**
명 칼

sword

7

◇ **attack**
동 공격하다
명 공격, 폭행
반 defend 방어하다

attack

8

◇ **bother**
동 괴롭히다

bother

9

◇ **opposite**
형 반대의

opposite

10

◇ **southern**
형 남쪽의
명 south 남쪽

southern

11

◇ **boastful**
형 자랑하는, 허풍 떠는
유 proud 자랑하는
반 humble 겸손한

boastful

12

▲ **coward**
명 겁쟁이
유 wimp 겁쟁이

coward

A 주어진 철자를 바르게 배열하여 빈칸에 알맞은 단어를 쓰세요.

1. renev → _____ to be late 결코 지각하지 않는
2. taatkc → a shark _____ 상어의 공격
3. dwsro → draw a _____ 칼을 뽑다
4. btroeh → _____ everybody 모두를 괴롭히다
5. cwroda → a soldier fighting like a _____ 겁쟁이처럼 싸우는 군인
6. lveea → _____ a message 메시지를 남기다
7. gntih → a dark _____ 어두운 밤
8. ioptsepo → in the _____ direction 반대 방향으로
9. aoeln → live _____ 혼자 살다
10. etbi → _____ your nails 손톱을 깨물다
11. tblofaus → a _____ liar 허풍 떠는 거짓말쟁이
12. stehonru → _____ wind 남풍

B 다음 장면에 어울리는 단어를 보기에서 골라 넣어 문장을 완성하세요.

> night   coward   attack   alone

1. I had a dream last _____ .
2. I was _____ in a cave.
3. A bat tried to _____ me.
4. But I'm not a _____ .
   I fought it instead of running away.

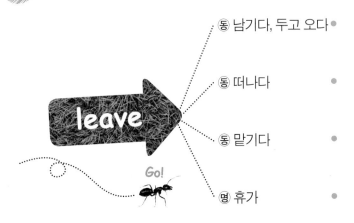

C 문장을 읽고, 빈칸에 알맞은 뜻을 쓴 후 해당하는 것을 선으로 연결하세요.

(동) 남기다, 두고 오다 •

(동) 떠나다 •

leave

Go!

(동) 맡기다 •

(명) 휴가 •

• <u>Leave</u> the ticket with me.
  티켓을 나에게 _____.

• I <u>leave</u> school at three.
  나는 학교를 3시에 _____.

• Can I take a <u>leave</u> on Friday?
  금요일에 _____ 를 내도 될까요?

• I <u>left</u> a book on the desk.
  나는 책을 책상 위에 _____.

D 문장을 읽고, 빈칸에 알맞은 단어를 쓰세요.

1. It's a summer _____. 여름 밤이다.

2. Ted is not a _____. 테드는 겁쟁이가 아니다.

3. So he goes out to look at the stars _____.
   그래서 그는 홀로 별들을 보러 밖으로 나간다.

4. He _____ a telescope on the table. 그는 망원경을 탁자 위에 둔다.

5. He _____ feels lonely in the dark. 어둠 속에서 그는 결코 외롭다고 느끼지 않는다.

6. He looks up at the dark _____ sky. 그는 어두운 남쪽 하늘을 올려다본다.

7. Big stars look like a _____ eagle. 큰 별들이 자랑하는 독수리 같다.

8. The _____ of boastful is modest. '자랑하는'의 반대말은 '겸손한'이다.

9. Some stars look like a _____. 어떤 별들은 칼처럼 보인다.

10. Some mosquitoes _____ him. 모기 몇 마리가 그를 괴롭힌다.

11. They _____ his arms and legs. 그것들은 그의 팔과 다리를 문다.

12. Crazy mosquitoes _____ him. 미친 모기들이 그를 공격한다.

Orion and the Scorpion

One summer _____,

Nick looks up at the s_____ sky.

Many groups of stars appear in the night sky.

Suddenly, he flies up into the sky with his dog.

He meets Orion high up in the sky.

Orion is a handsome but b_____ star.

He always _____ the other stars and teases the small stars.

Orion comes close to them.

"You are a _____. Your dog looks funny."

Nick is very angry. "Who says I'm a coward?

Just _____ us _____."

Nick's dog growls and rushes to bi_____ Orion.

Orion a_____ with his _____ and shield.

Nick shouts, "Help! They are having a big fight!"

Then, the stars of the scorpion show up.

The scorpion takes Orion to the winter sky.

The scorpion and Orion are placed on o_____ sides of the sky.

They have _____ met again in the night sky.

Word Box

night	southern	boastful	bothers	coward	leave
alone	bite	attacks	sword	opposite	never

Unit 8
Famous Places

The Moai on Easter Island

⭐ 초등 기본어휘 ⬡ 중등 기본어휘 ⬠ 확장어휘

1
⭐ **and**
졉 그리고

and

2
⭐ **how**
閉 어떻게

how

3
⭐ **heavy**
휑 무거운, (양·정도 등이) 많은[심한]
﨎 light 가벼운

heavy

4
⭐ **number**
졤 수

number

5
⬡ **bottom**
졤 아래
﨎 top 위
㋦ bottom line 핵심

bottom

6
⬡ **discover**
졩 발견하다
졤 discovery 발견

discover

7
⬡ **research**
졤 연구, 조사
졩 연구하다
㋧ study 연구

research

8
⬡ **attractive**
휑 매력적인 ㋧ charming 매력적인
졩 attract (흥미 등을) 끌다
졤 attraction 매력

attractive

9
⬠ **carve**
졩 조각하다, 새기다

carve

10
⬠ **statue**
졤 조각상

statue

11
⬠ **sleigh**
졤 썰매
㋧ sled 썰매; 썰매를 타다

sleigh

12
⬠ **heritage**
졤 유산

heritage

A 주어진 철자를 바르게 배열하여 빈칸에 알맞은 단어를 쓰세요.

1. hesecrar → do _____ 조사하다
2. who → _____ was your weekend? 주말 어떻게 보냈니?
3. varce → _____ a statue 조각상을 조각하다
4. embnur → a high _____ 큰 숫자
5. etctrataiv → an _____ woman 매력적인 여성
6. dan → bread _____ butter 버터 바른 빵
7. eatstu → stand like a _____ 조각상처럼 서있다
8. toobtm → the _____ line 핵심
9. iglseh → go _____ riding 썰매 타러 가다
10. yeavh → _____ rain 큰 비
11. ierthega → cultural _____ 문화유산
12. eisdcvor → _____ a new continent 새로운 대륙을 발견하다

B 연관되는 단어를 알아보고, 빈칸에 영어 또는 우리말 뜻을 쓰세요.

_____ snowfall
폭설
형 무거운, 심한 ⟷ 형 가벼운

the _____ on the song
그 노래에 대한 조사
명 연구, 조사 = 명 연구

an _____ woman
매력적인 여자
형 매력적인 = 형 매력적인

_____ new facts
새로운 사실들을 발견하다
동 발견하다 ⟹ 명 발견

C 빈칸에 알맞은 단어를 쓰고, 사다리를 타고 내려가 정답을 확인하세요.

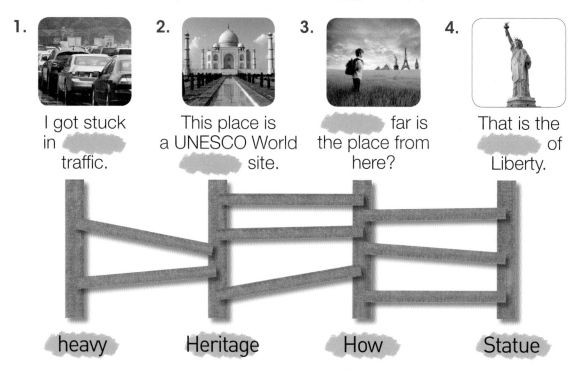

1. I got stuck in _____ traffic.

2. This place is a UNESCO World _____ site.

3. _____ far is the place from here?

4. That is the _____ of Liberty.

heavy　　　Heritage　　　How　　　Statue

D 문장을 읽고, 빈칸에 알맞은 단어를 쓰세요.

1. Who _____ this place?　누가 이 장소를 발견했을까?

2. The fantastic ice sculptures are _____ out of ice.
   환상적인 얼음 조각들이 얼음으로 조각되어 있다.

3. They look very _____.　그것들은 매우 매력적으로 보인다.

4. Children can also ride a _____ down the hill.
   어린이들은 또한 언덕 아래로 썰매를 타고 갈 수 있다.

5. At the _____ of the slope, they can have a snowball fight.
   경사면의 아래쪽에서 그들은 눈싸움을 할 수 있다.

6. _____ they can make snowmen with the snow.
   그리고 그들은 눈으로 눈사람들을 만들 수 있다.

7. _____ results show many kids want to visit this place.
   조사에 따르면, 많은 아이들이 이곳을 방문하고 싶어한다.

8. The _____ of visitors this winter will be over 100,000.
   이번 겨울 방문객의 수는 십만 명을 넘을 것이다.

The Moai* on Easter Island

Easter Island was _____ on Easter* Sunday in 1722.

It is famous for the large stone st_____ called moai.

Most of them are c_____ to show a body from the head down to the top of the thighs.

Only a small n_____ of them show a complete body kneeling.

The height of the statues ranges from 1 m to 30 m, _____ they weigh almost 20 tons each.

The _____ of the statues are hidden in the ground.

Can you guess _____ people moved these big statues?

They were so _____ that it was difficult for people to move them.

_____ shows there were lots of palm trees* on the island.

So people could have made sl_____ out of the palm trees to move them.

The moai, the stone statues on Easter Island, are so a_____.

Many tourists visit to see the world h_____ moai.

*moai 모아이(칠레 어스터 섬에 있는 미스테리한 석상들) Easter 부활절 palm tree 야자수

Word Box

bottoms Research statues sleighs how and

heritage discovered heavy carved number attractive

• Lesson 2 • Nick at the Pyramid

✪ 초등 기본어휘 ◇ 중등 기본어휘 ⬢ 확장어휘

1
✪ **loud**
형 소리가 큰, 시끄러운
유 noisy 시끄러운
부 loudly 큰 소리로

loud

2
✪ **speak**
동 말하다
유 say, talk, tell 말하다

speak

3
✪ **watch**
동 보다, (잠깐 동안) 봐주다, 조심하다
유 look at, see 보다
명 손목시계

watch

4
✪ **field trip**
명 현장 학습

field trip

5
✪ **black out**
구 기절하다, 깜깜하게 만들다
유 faint 기절하다
명 blackout 정전, 의식 상실

black out

6
◇ **exit**
명 출구   동 나가다
유 way out 출구
반 entrance 입구

exit

7
◇ **occur**
동 일어나다
유 happen, take place
일어나다

occur

8
◇ **backward**
부 뒤로
반 forward 앞으로

backward

9
◇ **exhibition**
명 전시
동 exhibit 전시하다

exhibition

10
◇ **come up to**
구 다가오다, (특정 지점까지) 오다

come up to

11
⬢ **scared**
형 겁먹은
유 afraid, frightened 겁이 난

scared

12
⬢ **mummy**
명 미라

mummy

A 주어진 철자를 바르게 배열하여 빈칸에 알맞은 단어를 쓰세요.

1. liefd ptri → the _____ _____ to the museum
   박물관으로 현장 학습

2. mcoe pu ot → They _____ _____ _____ me.
   그들이 내게로 다가온다.

3. yummm → the _____ movie   미라 영화

4. peksa → _____ well of him   그를 좋게 말하다

5. oxhetibiin → look forward to the _____   그 전시회를 기대하다

6. hawtc → _____ the baseball game   그 야구 경기를 보다

7. ucocr → _____ all over the world   전세계에서 발생하다

8. dolu → in a _____ voice   큰 목소리로

9. dcarse → _____ to death   겁이 나 죽을 것 같은

10. clabk uot → _____ _____ because of it   그것 때문에 기절하다

11. ixte → the _____ for this building   이 건물의 출구

12. acabwrkd → move _____   뒤로 움직이다

B 다음 장면에 어울리는 단어를 보기에서 골라 넣어 문장을 완성하세요.

speak	exhibition	scared	exit

1. There was a blackout at the [_____] hall in the museum.

2. The children are [_____] of the dark and start crying.

3. People [_____] louder to find others in the dark.

4. Everyone is trying to find the [_____].

C 문장을 읽고, 빈칸에 알맞은 뜻을 쓴 후 해당하는 것을 선으로 연결하세요.

(동) 보다, 지켜보다 •

(동) (잠깐 동안) 봐주다 •

watch

Go!

(동) 조심하다 •

(명) 손목시계 •

• I'm <u>watching</u> TV and eating popcorn.
나는 팝콘을 먹으며 TV를 _____.

• Your <u>watch</u> is under the desk.
네 _____는 책상 아래에 있다.

• <u>Watch</u> out for the dogs running around.
네 주변을 달리고 있는 개들을 _____.

• Would you <u>watch</u> my bag for a moment?
제 가방을 잠시 동안 _____실 수 있으세요?

D 문장을 읽고, 빈칸에 알맞은 단어를 쓰세요.

1. I went on a _____ _____ to a museum.
나는 박물관으로 현장 학습을 갔다.

2. An Egyptian _____ was being held there.   거기서는 이집트 전시가 열리고 있었다.

3. There were _____ which look alive.   살아있는 듯한 미라들이 있었다.

4. I was _____ them carefully.   나는 그것들을 주의깊게 보고 있었다.

5. Suddenly there was a _____ in the hall.   갑자기 홀 안이 정전이 되었다.

6. Everyone was _____ until an announcer _____, "Don't worry."   모든 사람들이 아나운서가 "걱정하지 마세요."라고 말할 때까지 겁에 질려 있었다.

7. I stepped _____.   나는 뒷걸음질 쳤다.

8. Then something strange _____. The mummies started to move.
그 때 이상한 일이 일어났다. 미라들이 움직이기 시작했다.

9. They _____ _____ _____ me.   그들이 나에게 다가왔다.

10. They were running towards the _____.   그들은 출구를 향해 뛰고 있었다.

11. I shouted as _____ as I could.   나는 할 수 있는 한 크게 소리 질렀다.

빈칸에 알맞은 단어를 단어 박스에서 찾아 넣어 이야기를 완성하세요.

Nick at the Pyramid*

Nick went on a _____ _____ to the museum.

He was left alone in the ancient Egypt e_____ room.

He tried to find the _____, but he fell down.

When he fell down, he _____ _____ in the museum.

Suddenly, Nick woke up. The wall made a _____ sound and began to move.

Nick was in a big, dark pyramid.

He was surprised to see _____.

He got s_____ and ran away, but there was no exit.

When he looked back, a surprising thing _____.

The mummies disappeared, and a Pharaoh* _____ _____ _____ Nick.

The Pharaoh _____ to Nick.

"_____ out, my new soldier. Come here."

At that moment, Nick stepped _____ and was back in the museum.

*pyramid 피라미드 **Pharaoh** 파라오(고대 이집트 국왕의 칭호)

Word Box

| Watch | came up to | field trip | mummies | loud | occurred |

| backward | exhibition | blacked out | exit | scared | spoke |

Unit 9
A Mysterious Plant

The Venus Flytrap

⭐ 초등 기본어휘 ◇ 중등 기본어휘 ⛰ 확장어휘

1
⭐ **if**
졉 만약 ~한다면

if

2
⭐ **poor**
형 빈약한, 가난한
반 rich 풍부한, 부자인
명 poverty 가난

poor

3
⭐ **wide**
부 활짝
형 넓은

wide

4
⭐ **short**
형 짧은
반 long 긴

short

5
⭐ **endanger**
동 위험에 빠뜨리다
명 danger 위험
형 dangerous 위험한

endanger

6
⭐ **greenhouse**
명 온실

greenhouse

7
◇ **allow**
동 허락하다, 인정하다
유 admit 허락하다

allow

8
◇ **mysterious**
형 신비한, 불가사의한
명 mystery 신비, 수수께끼

mysterious

9
⛰ **crawl**
동 엎드려 기다

crawl

10
⛰ **digest**
동 소화하다
명 digestion 소화
형 digestive 소화의

digest

11
⛰ **unlike**
전 ~와 다른
반 like ~와 같은

unlike

12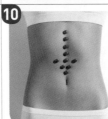
⛰ **nutrient**
명 영양소, 영양분

nutrient

A

주어진 철자를 바르게 배열하여 빈칸에 알맞은 단어를 쓰세요.

1. fi → _____ I were you 만약 내가 너라면
2. tenunitr → essential _____s 필수 영양소들
3. ropo → _____ condition 빈약한 조건
4. ousrtesmyi → _____ power 신비로운 힘
5. iwed → Open your eyes _____. 눈을 크게 떠라.
6. seehgrenou → _____ effect 온실 효과
7. wolal → _____ to go 가는 것을 허락하다
8. wcarl → A baby _____s. 아기가 엎드려 긴다.
9. ekulin → _____ others 다른 사람들과 달리
10. hotsr → _____ hair 짧은 머리
11. ergndaen → _____ his life 그의 생명을 위태롭게 하다
12. tisdge → _____ food 음식을 소화시키다

B

연관되는 단어를 알아보고, 빈칸에 영어 또는 우리말 뜻을 쓰세요.

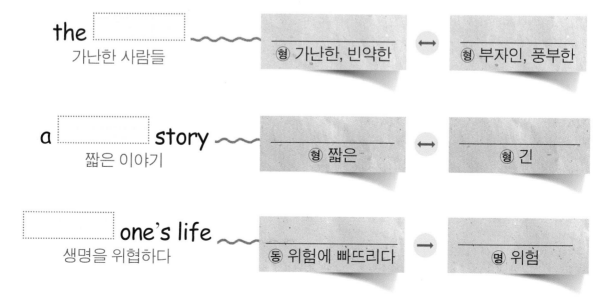

the [_____] 가난한 사람들 〜〜〜 _____ 형 가난한, 빈약한 ⟷ _____ 형 부자인, 풍부한

a [_____] story 짧은 이야기 〜〜〜 _____ 형 짧은 ⟷ _____ 형 긴

[_____] one's life 생명을 위협하다 〜〜〜 _____ 동 위험에 빠뜨리다 → _____ 명 위험

C 빈칸에 알맞은 단어를 쓰고, 사다리를 타고 내려가 정답을 확인하세요.

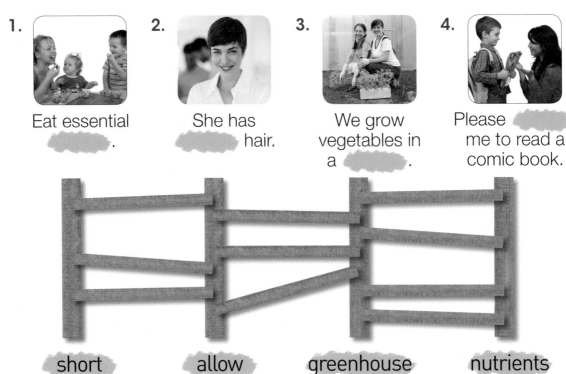

1. Eat essential _____.

2. She has _____ hair.

3. We grow vegetables in a _____.

4. Please _____ me to read a comic book.

short   allow   greenhouse   nutrients

D 문장을 읽고, 빈칸에 알맞은 단어를 쓰세요.

1. Today is sunny, _____ yesterday.   오늘은 어제와는 달리 화창하다.

2. I am an ant. I like to _____ on an apple.
   나는 개미다. 나는 사과 위를 기는 것을 좋아한다.

3. I have to open my mouth _____ to eat the apple.
   나는 사과를 먹기 위해서 입을 크게 벌려야 한다.

4. But I cannot _____ it.   하지만 나는 그것을 소화할 수 없다.

5. I don't like _____ soil.   나는 메마른 땅을 싫어한다.

6. It _____ ants.   그것은 개미들을 위험에 빠뜨린다.

7. My sister's ant likes _____ stories.
   나의 언니 개미는 신비한 이야기들을 좋아한다.

8. _____ she were a human, she would be a writer.
   그녀가 사람이라면 작가가 되었을 것이다.

E 빈칸에 알맞은 단어를 단어 박스에서 찾아 넣어 이야기를 완성하세요.

The Venus Flytrap

The Venus flytrap is a m_____ plant.

_____ other plants, it is an insect-eating plant.

It gets _____ from eating insects like ants, flies, or spiders.

The Venus flytrap lives in p_____ conditions in North and South Carolina.

People collect so many Venus flytraps that they have become

e_____.

So they are grown in _____ today.

The leaves of the Venus flytrap are usually open _____.

_____ hairs cover the leaves.

When an insect _____ on its leaves, its leaves close quickly.

The hairs and leaves don't _____ the insect to escape.

The Venus flytrap d_____ the soft,

inner parts of the insect.

_____ it swallows a stone or a nut,

the leaves reopen and spit it out.

This is the way the Venus flytrap lives.

Word Box

mysterious	wide	digests	poor	If	greenhouses
Unlike	Short	crawls	allow	nutrients	endangered

☆ 초등 기본어휘 ◇ 중등 기본어휘 ⬡ 확장어휘

1

☆ **die**
동 죽다
형 dead 죽은 명 death 사망
유 pass away 죽다

die

2

☆ **key**
명 비결, 열쇠
형 가장 중요한, 핵심적인

key

3

☆ **side**
명 쪽, 면

side

4

◇ **helpful**
형 도움이 되는
동 help 돕다
유 useful 쓸모 있는, 도움이 되는

helpful

5

☆ **lose one's footing**
구 발을 헛디디다

lose one's footing

6

◇ **gather**
동 모이다

gather

7

◇ **solution**
명 해결책, 해답
동 solve 문제를 해결하다

solution

8

◇ **troublesome**
형 골칫거리인

troublesome

9

◇ **get rid of**
구 ~을 없애다
유 remove 치우다, 제거하다

get rid of

10

⬡ **swamp**
명 늪, 습지
유 marsh 습지

swamp

11

⬡ **shovel**
명 삽

shovel

12

⬡ **tickle**
동 간질이다

tickle

A 주어진 철자를 바르게 배열하여 빈칸에 알맞은 단어를 쓰세요.

1. ied → _____ suddenly 갑자기 죽다
2. kictle → _____ a baby 아기를 간질이다
3. isde → left _____ 왼쪽 면
4. lufehlp → a _____ person 도움이 되는 사람
5. egt dir fo → _____ _____ _____ a bad smell
   나쁜 냄새를 없애다
6. nioutslo → a simple _____ 간단한 해결책
7. eky → the _____ to winning 승리의 비결
8. agerht → _____ in the living room 거실에 모이다
9. mesolebrtou → a _____ problem 골칫거리인 문제
10. sovhel → dig a hole with a _____ 삽으로 구멍을 파다
11. pwasm → a _____ tour 늪지 관광
12. olse → _____ one's footing 발을 헛디디다

B 다음 장면에 어울리는 단어나 구를 보기에서 골라 넣어 문장을 완성하세요.

| gather | helpful | key | get rid of |

1. People [ ] at the park. Look at the man on the bench.

2. How can he [ ] his stress?

3. Laughing is [ ].

4. It's the [ ] to being happy.

C 문장을 읽고, 빈칸에 알맞은 뜻을 쓴 후 해당하는 것을 선으로 연결하세요.

key Go!

(명) 비결 •

(명) 열쇠 •

(형) 핵심적인 •

• He has a gate key.
그가 출입문 _____를 가지고 있다.

• Good health is the key to happiness.
건강이 행복의 _____이다.

• What is the key sentence?
_____ 문장이 무엇입니까?

D 문장을 읽고, 빈칸에 알맞은 단어를 쓰세요.

1. We can find many animals in a _____ and a forest.
   우리는 늪지와 숲에서 많은 동물들을 발견할 수 있다.

2. Nature is _____ to wild animals.
   자연은 야생 동물들에게 도움이 된다.

3. Nowadays many animals _____ because of pollution.
   요즘은 오염 때문에 많은 동물들이 죽는다.

4. Pollution is _____.   오염은 골칫거리이다.

5. We want to _____ _____ _____ it.
   우리는 그것을 제거하고 싶다.

6. We think it is the _____ to helping nature.
   우리는 그것이 자연을 돕는 열쇠라고 생각한다.

7. So we _____ together to protect nature.
   그래서 우리는 자연을 보호하기 위해 함께 모인다.

8. Because cleaning up is the _____.   청소가 해결책이기 때문이다.

9. When I clean, my brother _____ my foot with a feather.
   내가 청소를 할 때 나의 남동생이 깃털로 나의 발을 간질인다.

10. I _____ _____ _____, so I fall.   나는 발을 헛디뎌서 넘어진다.

11. I use a _____ to stand up.   나는 삽을 이용해 일어난다.

12. One _____ of my body is covered in mud.   내 몸의 한쪽이 진흙으로 덮인다.

E 빈칸에 알맞은 단어를 단어 박스에서 찾아 넣어 이야기를 완성하세요.

A Helpful Plant

Nick and his friends _____ at Michelle's house.

Fruit flies* are flying around them.

"How can we _____ _____ _____ these fruit flies?

They're t_____."

Michelle says, "I have a _____. A Venus flytrap is the k_____.

Let's get a Venus flytrap."

They go to a _____ where the Venus flytrap grows.

Nick finds a Venus flytrap. It looks different from other Venus flytraps. It's very big.

At that moment, he _____ _____ _____ and slips.

"Look! The big Venus flytrap is swallowing Nick," cries Michelle.

"Pull the si_____ of the leaves. Hurry," shouts Grace.

Grace and Michelle try to open its leaves.

"I'm going to _____ it," says Justin.

The Venus flytrap spits Nick out.

"Whew~! I almost _____," says Nick.

They dig it out with a _____ and take it to Michelle's house.

The Venus flytrap catches all the fruit flies at Michelle's house.

What a _____ plant!

*fruit fly 초파리

Word Box

died   shovel   gather   helpful   swamp   solution

key   get rid of   sides   loses his footing   tickle   troublesome

Unit 10
The Guinness Book

• Lesson 1 • A Guinness World Record

☆ 초등 기본어휘 ○ 중등 기본어휘 ▲ 확장어휘

1
☆ **now**
　(부) 지금, 당장
now

2
☆ **who**
　(대) 누구
who

3
☆ **send**
　(동) (물건 등을) 보내다
send

4
○ **fact**
　(명) 사실, 실제
　(유) truth 진실
fact

5
○ **huge**
　(형) 거대한 (유) gigantic 거대한
　(비) huger 더 거대한
　(최) hugest 가장 거대한
huge

6
○ **detail**
　(동) 자세히 말하다
　(명) 자세한 설명
detail

7
○ **measure**
　(동) 재다, 측정하다,
　　(길이 등이) ～이다
measure

8
○ **apply**
　(동) 신청하다, 지원하다
apply

9
◇ **break a record**
　(구) 기록을 깨다
break a record

10
▲ **dwarf**
　(명) 난쟁이
　(복) dwarves 난쟁이들
　(반) giant 거인

dwarf

11
▲ **cockroach**
　(명) 바퀴벌레
cockroach

12
▲ **the same ～ as ...**
　(구) …와 같은 ～
the same ～ as...

A 주어진 철자를 바르게 배열하여 빈칸에 알맞은 단어를 쓰세요.

1. appyl → _____ for a piano contest 피아노 대회에 지원하다
2. won → here and _____ 여기 그리고 지금
3. adrvwse → Snow White and the 7 _____ 백설공주와 일곱 난쟁이들
4. how → _____ knows? 누가 알겠어?
5. uhgste → a _____ burger 가장 큰 버거
6. esnd → _____ a message 메시지를 보내다
7. kroachcoc → a _____ trap 바퀴벌레 덫
8. afct → get the _____s 사실들을 알아내다
9. maresue → _____ the classroom 교실 크기를 재다
10. eialtd → in _____ 자세하게, 상세하게
11. erodrc → break the _____ 그 기록을 깨다
12. eth asme → _____ _____ weight as an elephant
코끼리와 같은 무게

B 단어 뒤에 **-est**를 붙여 최상급 표현을 나타내요. 빈칸에 알맞은 최상급을 쓰세요.

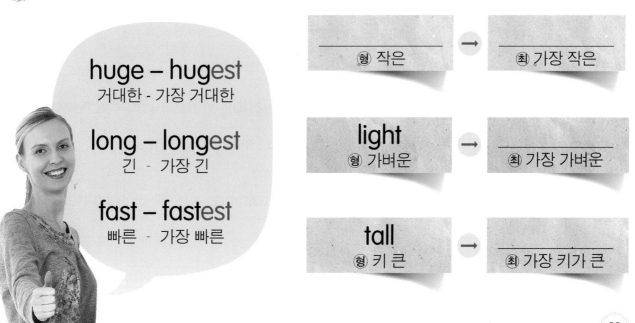

huge – hugest
거대한 - 가장 거대한

long – longest
긴 - 가장 긴

fast – fastest
빠른 - 가장 빠른

_____ (형) 작은 → _____ (최) 가장 작은

light (형) 가벼운 → _____ (최) 가장 가벼운

tall (형) 키 큰 → _____ (최) 가장 키가 큰

C 빈칸에 알맞은 단어를 쓰고, 사다리를 타고 내려가 정답을 확인하세요.

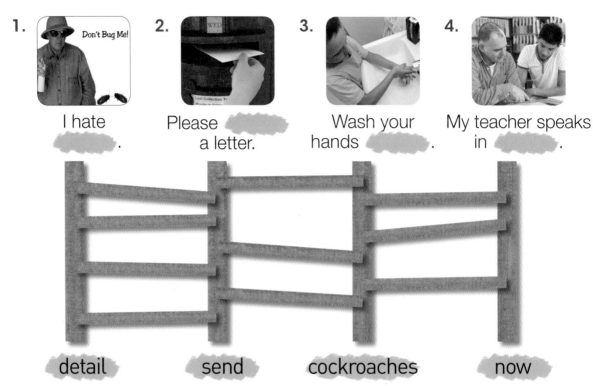

1. I hate _____ .

2. Please _____ a letter.

3. Wash your hands _____ .

4. My teacher speaks in _____ .

detail   send   cockroaches   now

D 문장을 읽고, 빈칸에 알맞은 단어를 쓰세요.

1. _____ are you? 당신은 누구죠?

2. I am one of Snow White's _____. 나는 백설공주의 난쟁이들 중 하나이다.

3. Don't _____ my height and weight. 나의 키와 몸무게를 측정하지 말아라.

4. As you can see, I'm short. That's a _____. 네가 보듯이 나는 작다. 그건 사실이다.

5. I know the _____ giant in the world. 나는 세상에서 가장 거대한 거인을 안다.

6. He _____ to be a runner at the Olympic Games.
   그는 달리기 선수로 올림픽에 참가를 신청했었다.

7. He had _____ _____ training _____ other normal
   people. 그는 다른 평범한 사람들과 같은 훈련을 받았다.

8. He trained very hard to _____ the world _____.
   그는 세계 기록을 깨기 위해서 아주 열심히 훈련했다.

 빈칸에 알맞은 단어를 단어 박스에서 찾아 넣어 이야기를 완성하세요.

A Guinness World Record

How big is the _____ pizza in the world?

It is about 37.4 m. That is _____ _____ size _____ a 10-story building.

How small is the smallest _____ in the world?

A cockroach in Japan _____ 9 mm long.

_____ is the world's lightest person?

It is a Mexican _____, who is 67 cm tall and weighs 2.14 kg.

We can find these _____ in the Guinness Book of World Records*.

It is a popular book that _____ the world's new records.

Does anyone want to _____ _____ world _____?

Try and then a_____ for a Guinness world record.

_____ your new record to the Guinness book.

Try it _____.

*Guinness Book of World Records 세계 기네스북

Word Box

Who | the same ~ as | facts | now | details | dwarf

measured | break a ~ record | hugest | Send | apply | cockroach

• Lesson 2 • Nick's World Record

★ 초등 기본어휘 ◇ 중등 기본어휘 △ 확장어휘

1 ★ tie
- 명 끈, 매듭
- 동 묶다

tie

2  ★ beef
- 명 소고기

beef

3 ★ chalk
- 명 분필

chalk

4 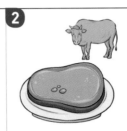 ★ continue
- 동 계속하다
- 유 go on 계속하다
- 형 continued 지속적인

continue

5  ★ in class
- 구 수업 중인

in class

6  ★ fall off
- 구 떨어지다

fall off

7  ★ button up
- 구 단추를 채워 잠그다
  (입·지갑 등을) 꼭 잠그다

button up

8  ◇ sore
- 형 아픈, 슬픔에 잠긴

sore

9  ◇ blame
- 동 혼내다, ~ 탓으로 돌리다
- 반 praise 칭찬하다

blame

10 ◇ upset
- 형 속상한, (위 따위에) 탈이 난
- 동 화나게 하다, 넘어뜨리다, 뒤집다

upset

11  ◇ medicine
- 명 약, 의약품
- *cf.* powder 가루약, pill 알약, liquid medicine 물약

medicine

12  ◇ disappoint
- 동 실망시키다

disappoint

A 주어진 철자를 바르게 배열하여 빈칸에 알맞은 단어를 쓰세요.

1. ediinecm → take _____ 약을 먹다
2. notuenicd → to be _____ 계속되다
3. eefb → _____ steak 소고기 스테이크
4. psetu → _____ with ~ 때문에 화가 나다
5. sreo → feel _____ 아픔을 느끼다
6. ite → _____ a bow 나비 모양으로 묶다
7. lbmea → Don't _____ him. 그를 혼내지 마라.
8. caklh → a piece of _____ 분필 하나
9. dpptioasin → You _____ ed me. 너는 나를 실망시켰다.
10. ni clssa → be _____ _____ 수업 중이다
11. utontb pu → _____ _____ my coat 나의 코트 단추를 잠그다
12. llaf fof → _____ _____ a sofa 소파에서 떨어지다

B 다음 장면에 어울리는 단어나 구를 보기에서 골라 넣어 문장을 완성하세요.

button up	fell off	tie

1. Mom, I can't _____ my shoes.

2. Just a minute. I'll help you, but can you try to _____ your shirt?

3. Okay. Oops! Mom, a button _____ .

C 문장을 읽고, 빈칸에 알맞은 뜻을 쓴 후 해당하는 것을 선으로 연결하세요.

(동) 화나게 하다 •

(형) 속상한 •

upset

Go!

(형) 탈이 난 •

• You <u>upset</u> me.
네가 나를 _____.

• I have an <u>upset</u> stomach.
나는 위가 _____.

• He was <u>upset</u> about his brother's bad behaviour.
그는 남동생의 나쁜 행동에 _____ 했다.

D 문장을 읽고, 빈칸에 알맞은 단어를 쓰세요.

1. Last night I _____ _____ the bed. 어제 나는 침대에서 떨어졌다.

2. So I have a _____ arm. 그래서 나는 팔이 아프다.

3. My mom _____ _____ my clothes for me.
엄마가 나를 위해 내 옷의 단추를 잠가주신다.

4. I have _____ soup for breakfast. 나는 아침으로 소고기국을 먹는다.

5. After breakfast I take some _____ for my arm.
아침 식사 후 나는 내 팔을 위해 약을 먹는다.

6. My teacher writes sentences with _____.
나의 선생님은 분필로 문장들을 쓰신다.

7. But I can't write the sentences _____ _____.
하지만 수업 시간에 나는 그 문장들을 쓸 수 없다.

8. My teacher doesn't get _____. 선생님은 화내지 않으신다.

9. My teacher asks us to _____ a ribbon in art class.
선생님께서 미술 시간에 우리들에게 리본을 묶으라고 하신다.

10. I cannot do that but my teacher is not _____ in me.
나는 그것을 할 수 없지만 선생님은 나에게 실망하지 않으신다.

11. He doesn't _____ me. 그는 나를 혼내지 않으신다.

12. I _____ studying very hard. 나는 계속해서 열심히 공부한다.

E 빈칸에 알맞은 단어를 단어 박스에서 찾아 넣어 이야기를 완성하세요.

Nick's World Record

Nick wants to break a Guinness world record.

Nick tries eating _____ as fast as he can.

He has an _____ stomach. So he takes some _____.

Nick practices throwing c_____ as far as he can.

He gets punished by his teacher for throwing chalk _____
_____.

Nick tries to b_____ u_____ his clothes quickly.

His mom _____ him because all of the buttons on his clothes
_____ _____.

He tries to _____ his shoes the fastest.

He gives up because his hands are _____.

Nick's really d_____. But Nick never gives up.

Nick will _____ to try to set a world record.

Word Box

| fall off | continue | disappointed | chalk | medicine | blames |

| in class | upset | button up | beef | tie | sore |

정답 및 해석

Unit 1
Personality
성격

• Lesson 1 • **Blood Type**　p.10

Ⓐ 1. both　　2. shy　　3. responsible　　4. social
5. careful　6. personality　7. end, end　8. goal
9. practical　10. give up　11. Everyone　12. focus

Ⓑ
a great personality
좋은 성격
= personality 형 성격, 개성 = character 형 성격

a little shy
조금 수줍어 하는
= shy 형 부끄러워 하는 = timid 형 소심한

everyone else
다른 모든 사람들
= everyone 대 모든 사람, 모두 = everybody 대 모든 사람

Ⓒ 1. goal　　2. both　　3. end　　4. focus

Ⓓ 1. personalities　2. Everyone　3. practical　4. gives up
5. responsible　6. careful　7. social　8. shy

Ⓔ **Blood Type**　p.13

<u>Everyone</u> has a blood type.
Your blood type is believed to influence your <u>personality</u>.
People with blood type A are <u>**shy**</u> and nervous.
They are very <u>**careful**</u>.
Blood type B people are very <u>**practical**</u>.
When they do something, they <u>**focus**</u> on it.
They try hard to reach their <u>**goal**</u> and work hard to the <u>**end**</u>.
People with blood type O are outgoing and <u>**social**</u>.
They also <u>**give up**</u> easily.
Blood type AB people are <u>**both**</u> shy and outgoing.
AB type people are <u>**responsible**</u>.
What is your blood type?
What is your personality like?

● 해석 ●
혈액형
모든 사람은 혈액형이 있다.
혈액형은 성격에 영향을 끼친다고 여겨진다.
혈액형이 A형인 사람들은 부끄러움을 타고 긴장을 잘한다.
그들은 매우 조심스럽다.

혈액형이 B형인 사람들은 대단히 현실적이다.
그들은 무언가를 할 때 그것에 집중한다.
그들은 자신들의 목표에 도달하려 열심히 노력하고 끝까지 열심히 한다.
혈액형이 O형인 사람들은 외향적이고 사교적이다.
그들은 또 쉽게 포기한다.
혈액형이 AB형인 사람들은 부끄러워하기도 하면서 외형적이기도 하다.
AB형 사람들은 책임감이 있다.
당신의 혈액형은 무엇인가?
당신의 성격은 어떤가?

• Lesson 2 • **New Classmates**　p.14

Ⓐ 1. kid　　2. like　　3. others　　4. classmate
5. answer　6. complain　7. tough　8. awful
9. selfish　10. naughty　11. borrow　12. tease

Ⓑ 1. kids　　2. classmates　　3. tease　　4. naughty

Ⓒ
like
동 좋아하다 → I can't swim like you.
나는 너 처럼 수영할 수가 없다.
전 ~ 같이, ~처럼 → I like you.
나는 너를 좋아한다.
Go! 전 ~하고 싶은 → My dad feels like dancing.
우리 아빠는 춤추고 싶어한다.

Ⓓ 1. classmate　2. awful　3. selfish　4. borrow
5. answered　6. like　7. tough　8. teased
9. naughty　10. Others　11. kid　12. complain

Ⓔ **New Classmates**　p.17
"Bang!"
"Mom, I'm home!"
Nick shouts in an angry voice.
Mom asks Nick, "How was your new school? How were your new <u>**classmates**</u>?"
"They are <u>**awful**</u>! My partner Justin is very <u>**selfish**</u>.
He said no when I asked to <u>**borrow**</u> a pencil.
Matthew is <u>**naughty**</u>. I gave the wrong <u>**answer**</u> in class.
Then, he <u>**teased**</u> me by saying, 'Don't you know the answer?' He did that in front of everyone. Grace <u>**complains**</u> over and over.
Mom, I really don't <u>**like**</u> this school. I want to go back to my old school."
Mom says, "I'm sure there is a good <u>**kid**</u>."
At that moment, Nick remembers a girl.

"Ah, a girl named Michelle was different from the **others**. She was kind. And her smile was lovely."

Mom says happily, "It's always **tough** on the first day. Everything will be all right. Cheer up, son."

● 해석 ●

새로운 반 친구들

"탕!"

"엄마, 저 왔어요!"

닉이 화난 목소리로 소리를 지른다.

엄마가 닉에게 묻는다. "새 학교는 어땠니? 새로운 반 친구들은 어땠어?"

"그들은 끔찍해요! 짝꿍인 저스틴은 매우 이기적이에요. 내가 연필을 빌려달라고 하니까 싫다고 했어요. 매튜는 장난이 심해요. 내가 수업 시간에 틀린 답을 말했어요. 그러니까, 그애가 '답을 몰라?'라고 말하면서 나를 놀렸어요. 그는 모두들 앞에서 그렇게 했어요. 그레이스는 계속 불평을 해요. 엄마, 난 이 학교가 정말 싫어요. 옛날 학교로 돌아가고 싶어요."

엄마가 말한다. "좋은 아이가 있을 거야."

바로 그 때, 닉은 한 소녀를 기억한다.

"아, 미셸이라는 여자 아이는 다른 아이들과 달랐어요. 그녀는 친절했어요. 그리고 미소가 사랑스러웠고요."

엄마는 기쁘게 말한다. "첫 날은 항상 힘들단다. 모든 것이 괜찮아질 거야. 기운 내라, 아들아."

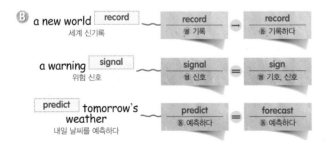

Unit 2

A Swimming Race
수영 대회

• Lesson 1 • **A Freestyle Swimming Race** p.18

Ⓐ 1. result   2. signal   3. best
4. neck and neck   5. record   6. predict
7. takes place   8. that   9. second
10. block   11. powerfully   12. catch up with

Ⓑ a new world [record] 세계 신기록 → | record 몡 기록 | ⇒ | record 통 기록하다 |

a warning [signal] 위험 신호 → | signal 몡 신호 | = | sign 몡 기호, 신호 |

[predict] tomorrow's weather 내일 날씨를 예측하다 → | predict 통 예측하다 | = | forecast 통 예측하다 |

Ⓒ 1. blocks   2. record   3. neck and neck
4. results

Ⓓ 1. took place   2. did their best   3. that

4. predict   5. signal   6. catch up with
7. powerfully, seconds

Ⓔ **A Freestyle Swimming Race** p.21

A 400 m freestyle swimming race is **taking place** now.

Five swimmers are at the starting **blocks**.

We expect **that** it will be a close race.

The swimmers are waiting for the starting **signal**.

"Bang!" They dive into the pool.

They are swimming **powerfully**.

Andrew turns first.

Mike and Robin turn after him.

Eric turns last.

All five swimmers **do their best**.

They are swimming **neck and neck**.

We cannot **predict** the **results** of this race.

Oh! Eric **catches up with** the other swimmers.

What a surprise! Eric is in the lead.

He touches the wall first. He is the winner.

He finishes in 3 minutes 58 **seconds**.

It's a new **record**. It was an exciting race.

● 해석 ●

자유형 수영 경기

400 미터 자유형 수영 경기가 지금 열리고 있다.

다섯 명의 수영 선수들이 출발대에 있다.

우리는 팽팽한 경기가 될 것으로 예상한다.

수영 선수들이 출발 신호를 기다리고 있다.

"탕!" 그들은 수영장 안으로 다이빙한다.

그들은 힘차게 수영을 하고 있다.

앤드류가 일등으로 턴을 한다.

마이크와 로빈이 그의 뒤를 이어 턴을 한다.

에릭이 마지막으로 턴을 한다.

다섯 명의 수영 선수들이 모두 최선을 다한다.

그들은 막상막하로 수영을 하고 있다.

우리는 이 경기의 결과를 예측할 수가 없다.

오! 에릭이 다른 수영 선수들을 따라잡는다.

놀라워라! 에릭이 선두에 선다.

그가 첫 번째로 들어온다. 그가 우승한다.

그는 3분 58초로 끝낸다.

이것은 신기록이다. 흥미진진한 경기였다.

• Lesson 2 • **Turtle, the Lifesaver** p.22

Ⓐ 1. lifesaver   2. save   3. than   4. toward
5. Go back   6. anymore   7. run away   8. turtle
9. left   10. splash   11. paddle   12. get a cramp

B 1. ran away   2. than   3. anymore   4. saved

C

D 1. went back   2. turtle   3. left   4. toward
5. saved   6. than   7. lifesaver   8. ran away
9. splashing   10. got a cramp   11. anymore
12. paddle

E Turtle, the Lifesaver   p.25

Nick and his friends found a **turtle** at the beach.
Nick tried to catch it, but the turtle **ran away** from him.
The turtle hurried and moved quickly **toward** the sea.
Nick followed it into the sea.
The turtle swam faster **than** Nick.
Justin shouted, "Nick, **splash** in the water."
Grace shouted, "**Paddle** with your hands."
Nick almost caught it.
Suddenly, he **got a cramp** in his foot.
He couldn't move his **left** foot.
So he couldn't swim **anymore**.
"Help! Help!" Nick slowly sank into the sea.
The turtle came up to Nick and carried him on his back.
The turtle took Nick to the beach.
"Turtle, thank you for **saving** me. You are a **lifesaver**."
The turtle smiled and **went back** into the sea.

● 해석 ●
거북이, 생명의 은인
닉과 그의 친구들은 해변에서 거북이 한 마리를 발견했다.
닉은 그것을 잡으려고 했는데 거북이가 그에게서 도망쳤다.
그 거북이는 서둘러서 바다를 향해 빨리 움직였다.
닉이 바다로 그것을 따라갔다.
거북이가 닉보다 더 빨리 수영을 했다.
저스틴이 소리쳤다. "닉, 물에서 첨벙거려."
그레이스가 소리쳤다. "손으로 물장구를 쳐."
닉이 거북이를 거의 따라잡았다.
갑자기, 닉의 발에 쥐가 났다.
그는 왼쪽 발을 움직일 수 없었다.
그래서 그는 더 이상 수영할 수가 없었다.
"도와줘! 도와줘!" 닉이 천천히 바다로 가라앉았다.
거북이가 닉에게 와서 닉을 등에 태웠다.
거북이가 닉을 해변으로 데리고 왔다.
"거북아, 나를 구해줘서 고마워. 너는 생명의 은인이야."
거북이는 웃으며 바다로 돌아갔다.

Unit 3
The Tallest Building
가장 높은 빌딩

• Lesson 1 • **Skyscraper**   p.26

A 1. Welcome   2. sway   3. skyscraper   4. million
5. strong   6. skyline   7. observation   8. height
9. steel   10. tall   11. city   12. company

B

C 1. steel   2. skyscraper   3. height   4. million

D 1. tall   2. height   3. company   4. steel
5. city   6. skyscrapers   7. millions   8. observation

E Skyscraper   p.29

Welcome to the Sears Tower in Chicago.
I'm Ted, a guide for this famous **skyscraper**.
This is one of the **tallest** buildings in the world.
Its **height** is about 440 meters.
It is made of **steel**.
It is **strong** enough to support 110 stories.
It is home to more than 100 **companies**.
Every year, 1.3 **million** tourists visit the Skydeck.
Let's take the elevator and go up to the Skydeck.
It only takes 60 seconds to get to the top.
Here is the **observation** deck.
The Skydeck is on the 103rd floor.
Can you feel how the building **sways** on this windy day?
Can you see far over the **city** and across Lake Michigan?
Look outside. The Chicago **skyline** is so wonderful.

● 해석 ●
고층 빌딩
시카고의 시어스 타워에 오신 것을 환영합니다.
저는 이 유명한 고층 빌딩의 가이드 테드입니다.

이것은 세계에서 가장 높은 빌딩 중 하나입니다.
이것의 높이는 약 440 미터입니다.
이것은 강철로 만들어졌습니다.
110층을 떠받치기에 충분히 강합니다.
여기에는 백여 개 이상의 회사가 들어서 있습니다.
해마다 백 삼십만 명의 관광객들이 스카이덱을 방문합니다.
엘리베이터를 타고 스카이덱으로 올라가시죠.
꼭대기까지 올라가는 데 60초밖에 걸리지 않습니다.
여기가 전망대입니다.
스카이덱은 103층에 있습니다.
이 바람 부는 날 빌딩이 흔들리는 것을 느끼시나요?
도시 멀리와 미시건 호수 너머가 보이시나요?
밖을 보세요. 시카고의 지평선은 정말 멋지답니다.

• Lesson 2 • **The Tower of Babel** p.30

Ⓐ 1. destroy 2. order 3. floor 4. storm
5. tornado 6. stone 7. collapse 8. into
9. dust 10. brick 11. heaven 12. quickly

Ⓑ 1. tornado 2. storm 3. collapse 4. quickly

Ⓒ
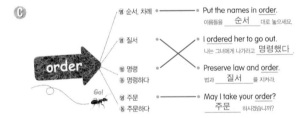

Ⓓ 1. floor 2. tornado 3. bricks, stones
4. into 5. orders 6. quickly 7. dust
8. collapses 9. storm 10. destroy, Heaven

Ⓔ **The Tower of Babel** p.33

One day, Nick sees a picture of a tall tower.
A **tornado** suddenly appears.
It takes him **into** the picture.
Some people are making **bricks** out of straw.
A director gives an **order** to Nick. "Carry the bricks to the tower."
An old man says, "Come on. Just drag them **quickly**."
The king shouts, "We will build the Tower of Babel.
The tower will go high up into **heaven**."
Nick says, "Oh, no. You need strong **stones** and wood to support it."
Soon, a **storm** is blowing angrily.

The tower **collapses** in a cloud of smoke.
People scream and are covered in **dust**.
Nick drops down on the **floor** from the picture.
Now, the Tower of Babel is **destroyed**.

● 해석 ●
바벨탑
어느 날, 닉은 높은 탑 그림을 본다.
토네이도가 갑자기 일어난다.
그것은 닉을 그림 속으로 데려간다.
어떤 사람들은 지푸라기로 벽돌을 만들고 있다.
감독관이 닉에게 명령을 내린다. "벽돌들을 탑으로 옮겨라."
한 노인이 "어서. 그것들을 빨리 끌고 와."라고 말한다.
왕이 소리를 친다. "우리는 바벨탑을 지을 거야. 이 탑은 하늘까지 높이 올라갈 거야."
닉은 "어, 안돼요. 그것을 떠받칠 강한 돌과 나무가 필요해요."라고 말한다.
곧 폭풍이 강하게 불어온다.
탑은 연기 구름 속에서 무너진다.
사람들은 비명을 지르며 먼지로 뒤덮인다.
닉은 그림에서 마룻바닥으로 떨어진다.
이제, 바벨탑은 파괴되었다.

Unit 4 **Paper World** 종이 세상

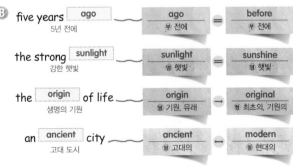

• Lesson 1 • **Papyrus** p.34

Ⓐ 1. wetland 2. part 3. origin 4. sheet
5. strip 6. ago 7. ancient 8. No
9. sunlight 10. soak 11. century 12. then

Ⓑ
five years **ago** / ago 전에 = before 전에
the strong **sunlight** / sunlight 햇빛 = sunshine 햇빛
the **origin** of life / origin 기원, 유래 → original 최초의, 기원의
an **ancient** city / ancient 고대의 → modern 현대의

C 1. Wetlands　2. no　3. century　4. Soak

D 1. ago　2. origin　3. strips　4. sunlight
　5. parts　6. ancient　7. then　8. sheet

E **Papyrus**　p.37

Papyrus is a plant which grows in **wetlands**.
It is also the world's first paper.
It was used by the **ancient** Egyptians.
Can you imagine if there was **no** paper in the world?
We can't imagine a world without paper.
How did the Egyptians make paper thousands of years **ago**?
They peeled off the outer **part** of the papyrus plant.
They cut the inner part into thin **strips**.
Next, they **soaked** the papyrus plant strips in water.
Then, what do you think happened?
They flattened the strips into **sheets**.
Lastly, the sheets were dried in the **sunlight**.
The **origin** of the word "paper" comes from "papyrus."
Papyrus was used until the 8th **century**.

● 해석 ●
파피루스
파피루스는 습지에서 자라는 식물이다.
세계 최초의 종이이기도 하다.
그것은 고대 이집트인들에 의해서 사용되었다.
세상에 종이가 없었다면 하고 상상할 수 있는가?
우리는 종이 없는 세상을 상상할 수 없다.
이집트인들은 수 천년 전에 어떻게 종이를 만들었을까?
그들은 파피루스 식물의 바깥 쪽 부분의 껍질을 벗겼다.
그들은 안쪽 부분을 얇고 가는 조각들로 잘랐다.
다음에 그들은 파피루스 식물 조각들을 물에 적셨다.
그러고 나서, 무슨 일이 일어났다고 생각하는가?
그들은 그 가느다란 조각들을 평평하게 펴서 시트로 만들었다.
마지막으로, 그 시트들은 햇빛에 건조되었다.
'종이'라는 말의 기원은 '파피루스'에서 왔다.
파피루스는 8세기까지 사용되었다.

• Lesson 2 • **Magic Drawing Paper** p.38

A 1. pop out　2. wave　3. rub　4. art class
　5. look around　6. erase
　7. drawing paper　8. Listen　9. everything
　10. realize　11. sketch　12. give, out light

B 1. art class　2. listening　3. sketch
　4. drawing paper

C

D 1. art class　2. sketching　3. erase　4. rub
　5. drawing paper　6. everything　7. look around
　8. wave　9. Listen　10. gives out light
　11. pops out　12. realize

E **Magic Drawing Paper**　p.41

Nick has **art class** outdoors.
Today's activity is to draw the area around his school.
Nick is **sketching** trees and rides in the playground.
He **erases** parts of a tall tree.
So, the tree **gives out light**.
Then, he falls on a white floor.
Everything around him is white.
When he sees the tall tree, he **realizes** that he is in the paper.
He wants to get out of the **drawing paper**.
Nick climbs up the tall tree and **looks around**.
"Is anybody here? **Listen** to me!"
Nick shouts and **waves** his hands.
Nick's friends Justin and Michelle are looking for him.
They hear Nick's voice and find him in the drawing paper.
Justin draws a door and **rubs** the paper.
Then, the door opens, and poor Nick **pops out** of the paper.

● 해석 ●
마법의 도화지
닉은 야외에서 미술 수업을 한다.
오늘 활동은 학교 주변 지역을 그리는 것이다.
닉은 운동장에 있는 나무들과 놀이기구들을 스케치하고 있다.
그는 큰 나무의 일부분을 지운다.
그러자 나무가 빛을 낸다.
그러고 나서, 그가 하얀 마루 위에 떨어진다.
그의 주변에 있는 모든 것들이 하얀색이다.
큰 나무를 보면서 그는 자신이 종이 안에 있다는 것을 깨닫는다.
그는 도화지 밖으로 나가고 싶다.
닉은 큰 나무 위로 올라가서 주변을 둘러본다.
"여기 누구 없어요? 내 말 좀 들어봐요!"
닉이 소리치면서 손을 흔든다.
닉의 친구인 저스틴과 미셸이 그를 찾고 있다.
그들은 닉의 목소리를 듣고 도화지에서 그를 찾는다.
저스틴은 문을 그리고 그 종이를 문지른다.

그러자, 문이 열리고 불쌍한 닉이 종이 밖으로 튀어나온다.

Unit 5
Water Changes
물의 변화

• Lesson 1 • **The Water Cycle**   p.42

Ⓐ
1. or   2. form   3. up   4. rise
5. down   6. water drop   7. River   8. water cycle
9. heat   10. water vapor   11. flow   12. surface

Ⓑ
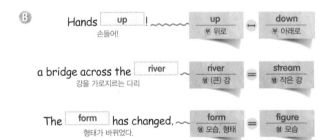

Hands [up]!   [up 부 위로] ⟷ [down 부 아래로]
손들어!

a bridge across the [river]   [river 형 (큰) 강] = [stream 형 작은 강]
강을 가로지르는 다리

The [form] has changed.   [form 형 모습, 형태] = [figure 형 모습]
형태가 바뀌었다.

Ⓒ
1. rises   2. heat   3. surface   4. flows

Ⓓ
1. or   2. water cycle   3. form   4. up
5. Water vapor   6. river   7. water drop
8. down

Ⓔ **The Water Cycle**   p.45

70% of the Earth's **surface** is water.
The sun shines on the **river**.
It **heats** the water.
Water becomes **water vapor**.
Water vapor **rises** from the river.
It goes **up** into the sky.
Water vapor gets cold and becomes **water drops**.
Water drops come together and **form** clouds.
Water drops in the clouds come back to earth.
They fall into the rivers as rain **or** snow.
Water flows **down** from upper streams.
The rivers **flow** into the oceans.
And the **water cycle** begins again.

● 해석 ●

물의 순환
지구 표면의 70 퍼센트는 물이다.
태양은 강 위를 비춘다.
그것은 물을 데운다.
물은 수증기가 된다.
수증기는 강에서부터 올라간다.
그것은 하늘로 올라간다.
수증기는 차가워져서 물방울이 된다.
물방울들은 함께 구름을 형성한다.
구름 속의 물방울들은 땅으로 돌아온다.
그것들은 비나 눈으로 강으로 떨어진다.
물은 상류에서 아래로 흐른다.
강들은 바다로 흐른다.
그리고 물의 순환은 다시 시작한다.

• Lesson 2 • **A Wonderful Experience** p.46

Ⓐ
1. cover   2. turn into   3. lot of   4. evaporate
5. cool   6. chilly   7. freeze   8. each other
9. Ocean   10. Lighten   11. person   12. sheep

Ⓑ
1. sheep   2. covered   3. a lot of   4. lightens

Ⓒ
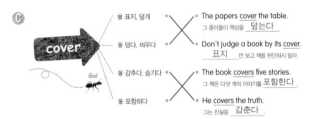

cover

Go!

형 표지, 덮개 → The papers cover the table.
그 종이들이 책상을 [덮는다].

덮다, 씌우다 → Don't judge a book by its cover.
[표지]만 보고 책을 판단하지 말라.

감추다, 숨기다 → The book covers five stories.
그 책은 다섯 개의 이야기를 [포함한다].

통 포함하다 → He covers the truth.
그는 진실을 [감춘다].

Ⓓ
1. a lot of   2. cool   3. lightens   4. turns into
5. covered   6. sheep   7. each other   8. chilly
9. frozen   10. person   11. evaporate   12. ocean

Ⓔ **A Wonderful Experience**   p.49

It is a cloudy day.
The sky is **covered** with clouds.
The clouds look like a flock of **sheep**.
Nick closes his eyes and lies on a tube in the **ocean**.
Nick feels his body **lighten**.
When he opens his eyes, he **turns into** water.
He **evaporates** and goes up into the sky.
He has **a lot of** friends in the sky.
It is very **chilly** in the sky.
Nick and his friends hug **each other**.

They **freeze** and become snow.

They feel heavy, so they fall down into the ocean.

At that moment, Nick turns into a **person** again.

"Wow! That was so **cool**! It was such a wonderful experience."

● 해석 ●

멋진 경험

흐린 날이다.

하늘이 구름들로 덮여 있다.

구름들이 양떼처럼 생겼다.

닉은 눈을 감고 바다에 있는 튜브 위에 누워 있다.

닉은 몸이 가벼워지는 것을 느낀다.

눈을 뜨자 그는 물이 된다.

그는 증발해서 하늘로 올라간다.

하늘에는 많은 친구들이 있다.

하늘은 매우 춥다.

닉과 그의 친구들은 서로 껴안는다.

그들은 얼어서 눈이 된다.

그들은 무거워진 것처럼 느끼더니 바다로 떨어진다.

그때, 닉은 다시 사람으로 바뀐다.

"와! 멋졌어! 아주 멋진 경험이었어."

Unit 6
About Junk Food
정크 푸드에 대해서

• Lesson 1 • **Fast Food**   p.50

Ⓐ 1. movie   2. meal   3. offer   4. quit

5. treatment   6. as   7. limit   8. distance

9. weight   10. test   11. throw up   12. depression

Ⓑ

show a [movie] ～～～ | movie 명 영화 | = | film 명 영화 |
영화를 상영하다

[offer] a preference ～～～ | offer 동 제공하다, 제안하다 | = | suggest 동 제안하다 |
우선권을 제공하다

[test] your memory ～～～ | test 동 시험하다, 검사하다 | → | test 명 시험 |
당신의 기억력을 시험하다

[quit] my job ～～～ | quit 동 그만두다 | = | give up 관 포기하다 |
나의 일을 그만두다

Ⓒ 1. lose   2. offers   3. meal   4. limit

Ⓓ 1. movie   2. as   3. distance   4. quit

5. throwing up   6. testes   7. treatment

8. depressed

Ⓔ **Fast Food**   p.53

Morgan Spurlock made the **movie** *Super Size Me*.

He **tested** the bad effects of fast food on himself.

He carried out a program **as** follows.

1. He ate three **meals** a day at a fast-food restaurant for thirty days.

2. If a restaurant worker **offered** to supersize the meal, he accepted the offer.

3. He **limited** himself to walking 1~2 km a day.
   That is the average **distance** Americans walk daily.

He got **treatment** from a doctor regularly during his program.

He **threw up** after eating fast food 4 days later.

His **weight** increased from 85 kg to 96 kg in a month.

He also got symptoms of **depression** and high blood pressure.

To be healthy again, he had to **quit** eating fast food.

● 해석 ●

패스트푸드

모간 스펄록은 '수퍼 사이즈 미'라는 영화를 만들었다.

그는 스스로 패스트푸드의 악영향들을 시험했다.

그는 다음과 같은 프로그램을 실행했다.

1. 그는 30일 동안 패스트푸드점에서 하루 세끼를 먹었다.

2. 음식점 종업원이 음식을 특대로 하는 것을 제안하면 그는 그 제안을 받아들였다.

3. 그는 걷는 것을 하루에 1~2 킬로미터로 제한한다. 그것은 미국인들이 매일 걷는 평균 거리이다.

그는 프로그램을 하는 동안 규칙적으로 의사에게 치료를 받았다.

그는 패스트푸드를 먹은 4일 뒤에 토했다.

그의 몸무게는 한 달만에 85 킬로그램에서 96 킬로그램으로 증가했다.

그는 또 우울증과 고혈압 증상을 보였다.

다시 건강해지기 위해 그는 패스트푸드를 먹는 것을 그만둬야 했다.

• Lesson 2 • **Burger Fighting**   p.54

Ⓐ 1. fresh   2. human   3. remove   4. woman

5. hate   6. snatch   7. already   8. friendship

9. regret   10. fell under a spell   11. way

12. today

Ⓑ 1. women   2. on the way home   3. regret

4. hate

ⓒ

형 방식
I want to buy a one-way ticket to Seoul.
나는 서울로 가는 한 ___방향___ 티켓을 사고 싶다.

형 길
Can you tell me the way to the shopping mall?
내게 쇼핑몰로 가는 ___길___ 을 알려줄 수 있니?

형 방향
This bag is way better than that one.
이 가방이 저것보다 ___훨씬___ 좋다.

부 훨씬
I don't like the way she looks at me.
나는 그녀가 나를 보는 ___방식___ 이 맘에 안 든다.

ⓓ 1. friendship　　2. hates　　3. snatches
4. falls under a spell　　5. fresh　　6. today
7. woman　　8. way　　9. already　　10. human
11. removes　　12. regrets

ⓔ **Burger Fighting**　　p.57

Nick didn't feel well **today**.

Nick and Matthew were eating burgers on their **way** home.

Nick **snatched** Matthew's burger to eat some more.

"You're so bad. I **hate** you!" shouted Matthew.

An old **woman** dropped her fruit basket in front of them.

Nick picked up the fruit and gave it to her.

She thanked Nick and gave him some **fresh** fruit.

When he ate a peach, his body changed into a burger.

He found Matthew, but Matthew had **already** become a burger.

Nick and Matthew **fell under a spell** because of their fight.

When they **regretted** fighting, the old woman appeared.

She made sure that their **friendship** was still strong.

So she **removed** the spell.

They changed back into **humans** again.

They promised not to fight anymore.

● 해석 ●
버거 싸움
닉은 오늘 기분이 좋지 않았다.
닉과 매튜는 집에 오는 길에 버거를 먹고 있었다.
닉은 조금 더 먹기 위해 매튜의 버거를 낚아챘다.
"너 정말 나쁘구나. 난 네가 싫어!"라고 매튜가 소리쳤다.
어느 늙은 여자가 그녀의 과일 바구니를 그들 앞에 떨어뜨렸다.
닉은 과일을 주워 그녀에게 주었다.
그녀는 닉에게 고마워하며 그에게 신선한 과일을 좀 주었다.
그가 복숭아를 먹자 그의 몸이 버거로 변했다.
그는 매튜를 찾았지만 매튜는 이미 버거가 되어 있었다.
닉과 매튜는 싸움 때문에 주문에 걸렸다.
그들이 싸운 것을 후회했을 때, 그 늙은 여자가 나타났다.
그녀는 그들의 우정이 여전히 강하다고 확신했다.
그래서 그녀는 주문을 풀어주었다.
그들은 다시 사람으로 돌아왔다.
그들은 더 이상 싸우지 않기로 약속했다.

Unit 7
The Seven Stars
일곱 개의 별들

● Lesson 1 ● **The Big Dipper**　　p.58

Ⓐ 1. once　　2. bowl　　3. almost　　4. wagon
5. direction　　6. constellation　　7. round　　8. ox
9. northern　　10. sailor　　11. position　　12. describe

Ⓑ
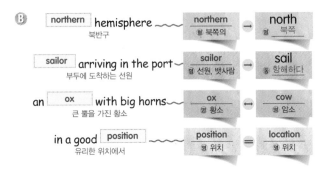

northern hemisphere 북반구 → northern 형 북쪽의 → north 형 북쪽

sailor arriving in the port 부두에 도착하는 선원 → sailor 형 선원, 뱃사람 → sail 동 항해하다

an ox with big horns 큰 뿔을 가진 황소 → ox 형 황소 ⇄ cow 형 암소

in a good position 유리한 위치에서 → position 형 위치 = location 형 위치

ⓒ 1. round　　2. bowl　　3. almost　　4. direction

ⓓ 1. sailors　　2. almost　　3. northern　　4. oxen
5. once　　6. bowls　　7. constellation　　8. describe

ⓔ **The Big Dipper**　　p.61

Have you ever seen stars in the sky?

Look at a group of stars in the **northern** part of the sky.

Almost everybody can find seven bright stars in a group.

They form the third largest **constellation**.

People call it different names, including the Big Dipper.

The ancient Greeks **described** it as a bear with a long tail.

The Romans believed that the stars looked like seven **oxen**.

The Vikings thought it was a **wagon** traveling in the sky.

The native Americans said it looked like a **bowl** with a bent handle.

When ancient **sailors** lost their way, the Big Dipper guided them in the right **direction**.

They could tell the time by looking at the **position** of the Big Dipper.

It appears to circle **round** the North star, Polaris, **once** a night.

해석

북두칠성

하늘의 별들을 본 적이 있나?

북쪽 하늘의 별무리를 보라.

거의 모든 사람들이 일곱 개의 밝은 별 한 무리를 찾을 수 있다.

그것들은 세 번째로 큰 별자리를 형성한다.

사람들은 그것을 북두칠성을 포함해서 다른 이름들로 부른다.

고대 그리스인들은 그것을 긴 꼬리를 가진 곰이라고 묘사했다.

로마인들은 그 별들이 일곱 마리의 황소처럼 보인다고 믿었다.

바이킹들은 그것을 하늘을 여행하는 마차라고 생각했다.

북미 원주민들은 그것을 구부러진 손잡이가 달린 그릇처럼 보인다고 말했다.

옛날 뱃사람들이 길을 잃었을 때, 북두칠성이 그들을 올바른 방향으로 안내해 주었다.

그들은 북두칠성의 위치를 보고 시간을 분간할 수 있었다.

그것은 하룻밤에 한 번 나타나서 북극성인 폴라리스의 둘레를 돈다.

• Lesson 2 • **Orion and the Scorpion** p.62

Ⓐ 1. never　　2. attack　　3. sword　　4. bother

5. coward　　6. leave　　7. night　　8. opposite

9. alone　　10. bite　　11. boastful　　12. southern

Ⓑ 1. night　　2. alone　　3. attack　　4. coward

Ⓒ
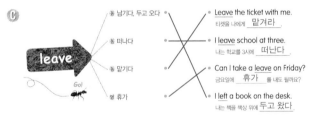

동 남기다, 두고 오다 ── Leave the ticket with me.
티켓을 나에게 맡겨라

동 떠나다 ── I leave school at three.
나는 학교를 3시에 떠난다

동 맡기다 ── Can I take a leave on Friday?
금요일에 휴가 를 내도 될까요?

명 휴가 ── I left a book on the desk.
나는 책을 책상 위에 두고 왔다

Ⓓ 1. night　　2. coward　　3. alone　　4. leaves

5. never　　6. southern　　7. boastful　　8. opposite

9. sword　　10. bother　　11. bite　　12. attack

Ⓔ **Orion and the Scorpion**　p.65

One summer <u>night</u>, Nick looks up at the <u>southern</u> sky.

Many groups of stars appear in the night sky.

Suddenly, he flies up to the sky with his dog.

He meets Orion high up into the sky.

Orion is a handsome but **boastful** star.

He always <u>bothers</u> the other stars and teases the small stars.

Orion comes close to them. "You are a <u>coward</u>. Your dog looks funny."

Nick is very angry. "Who says I'm a coward? Just <u>leave</u>

us **alone**."

Nick's dog growls and rushes to **bite** Orion.

Orion **attacks** with his <u>sword</u> and shield.

Nick shouts, "Help! They are having a big fight!"

Then, the stars of the scorpion show up.

The scorpion takes Orion to the winter sky.

The scorpion and Orion are placed on **opposite** sides of the sky.

They have <u>never</u> met again in the night sky.

해석

오리온과 전갈

어느 여름밤, 닉은 남쪽 하늘을 올려다본다.

많은 별 무리들이 밤하늘에 나타난다.

갑자기, 그는 개와 함께 하늘로 날아오른다.

그는 높은 하늘에서 오리온을 만난다.

오리온은 잘생겼지만 잘난 척하는 별이다.

그는 항상 다른 별들을 괴롭히고 작은 별들을 놀린다.

오리온이 그들에게 가까이 온다. "너는 겁쟁이야. 네 개는 웃기게 생겼어."

닉은 아주 화가 난다. "누가 나를 겁쟁이라고 하는 거야? 우리를 그냥 내버려둬."

닉의 개는 으르렁거리며 오리온을 물려고 달려든다.

오리온은 그의 칼과 방패로 공격한다.

닉이 소리친다. "도와줘요! 이들이 큰 싸움을 해요!"

그러자 전갈 별자리가 나타난다.

전갈은 오리온을 겨울 하늘로 데려간다.

전갈과 오리온은 반대쪽 하늘에 놓인다.

그들은 밤하늘에서 다시는 만나지 않았다.

Unit 8

Famous Places

유명한 장소들

• Lesson 1 • **The Moai on Easter Island** p.66

Ⓐ 1. research　　2. How　　3. carve　　4. number

5. attractive　　6. and　　7. statue　　8. bottom

9. sleigh　　10. heavy　　11. heritage　　12. discover

Ⓑ

heavy snowfall 폭설	heavy 형 무거운, 심한	⟺	light 형 가벼운
the research on the song 그 노래에 대한 조사	research 형 연구, 조사	=	study 형 연구
an attractive woman 매력적인 여자	attractive 형 매력적인	=	charming 형 매력적인
discover new facts 새로운 사실들을 발견하다	discover 동 발견하다	→	discovery 형 발견

정답 및 해석

C 1. heavy 2. Heritage 3. How 4. Statue

D 1. discovered 2. carved 3. attractive 4. sleigh
5. bottom 6. And 7. Research 8. number

E **The Moai on Easter Island** p.69

Easter Island was **discovered** on Easter Sunday in 1722.
It is famous for the large stone **statues** called moai.
Most of them are **carved** to show a body from the head
down to the top of the thighs.
Only a small **number** of them show a complete body
kneeling.
The height of the statues ranges from 1 m to 30 m, **and**
they weigh almost 20 tons each.
The **bottoms** of the statues are hidden in the ground.
Can you guess **how** people moved these big statues?
They were so **heavy** that it was difficult for people to
move them.
Research shows there were lots of palm trees on the
island.
So people could have made **sleighs** out of the palm trees
to move them.
The moai, the stone statues on Easter Island, are so
attractive.
Many tourists visit to see the world **heritage** moai.

● 해석 ●
이스터 섬의 모아이
이스터 섬은 1722년 일요일이었던 부활절에 발견되었다.
이곳은 모아이라는 커다란 석상들로 유명하다.
그것들 대부분은 머리에서 허벅지 위까지 몸이 보이게 조각되었다.
그것들 중 적은 수만이 무릎을 꿇고 있는 몸 전체를 보여준다.
조각상들의 높이는 1 미터에서 30 미터까지이고, 무게는 각각 거의 20 톤
에 이른다.
조각상들의 아랫부분은 땅에 숨겨져 있다.
사람들이 어떻게 이렇게 큰 조각상들을 움직였었는지 유추해 볼 수 있는가?
그것들은 너무 무거워서 사람들이 움직이기 어려웠다.
조사에 의하면 그 섬에는 많은 야자수가 있었다.
그래서 사람들은 그것들을 움직일 수 있게 야자수로 썰매를 만들수 있었다.
이스터 섬의 석상들인 모아이는 아주 매력적이다.
많은 관광객들이 세계 유산인 모아이를 보기 위해 방문한다.

• Lesson 2 • **Nick at the Pyramid** p.70

A 1. field trip 2. come up to 3. mummy 4. speak
5. exhibition 6. watch 7. occur 8. loud
9. scared 10. black out 11. exit 12. backward

B 1. exhibition 2. scared 3. speak 4. exit

C

통 보다, 지켜보다 ──── I'm **watching** TV and eating popcorn.
나는 팝콘을 먹으며 TV를 보고 있다.

통 (잠깐 동안) 봐주다 ──── Your **watch** is under the desk.
네 손목시계 는 책상 아래에 있다.

통 조심하다 ──── **Watch** out for the dogs running around.
네 주변을 달리고 있는 개들을 조심해라.

명 손목시계 ──── Would you **watch** my bag for a moment?
제 가방을 잠시 동안 봐주 실 수 있으세요?

D 1. field trip 2. exhibition 3. mummies 4. watching
5. blackout 6. scared, spoke 7. backward
8. occurred 9. came up to 10. exit 11. loud

E **Nick at the Pyramid** p.73

Nick went on a **field trip** to the museum.
He was left alone in the ancient Egypt **exhibition** room.
He tried to find the **exit**, but he fell down.
When he fell down, he **blacked out** in the museum.
Suddenly, Nick woke up. The wall made a **loud** sound
and began to move.
Nick was in a big, dark pyramid.
He was surprised to see **mummies**.
He got **scared** and ran away, but there was no exit.
When he looked back, a surprising thing **occurred**.
The mummies disappeared, and a Pharaoh **came up to**
Nick.
The Pharaoh **spoke** to Nick. "**Watch** out, my new soldier.
Come here."
At that moment, Nick stepped **backward** and was back
in the museum.

● 해석 ●
피라미드 안의 닉
닉은 박물관으로 현장 학습을 갔다.
그는 고대 이집트 전시실에 혼자 남겨졌다.
그는 출구를 찾으려 했지만 넘어졌다.
그가 넘어졌을 때, 박물관에서 기절했다.
갑자기, 닉이 깨어났다. 벽이 큰 소리를 내더니 움직이기 시작했다.
닉은 크고 캄캄한 피라미드 안에 있었다.
그는 미라들을 보고 놀랐다.
그는 무서워서 도망쳤지만 비상구가 없었다.
그가 뒤를 돌아봤을 때, 놀라운 일이 일어났다.
미라들이 사라지고 파라오가 닉에게 다가왔다.
파라오는 닉에게 말했다. "조심해라, 내 새로운 병사여. 이리로 오거라."
그 순간, 닉이 뒤로 물러나자 박물관으로 돌아와 있었다.

100

Unit 9
A Mysterious Plant
신비로운 식물

• Lesson 1 • The Venus Flytrap   p.74

A 1. if   2. nutrient   3. poor   4. mysterious
5. wide   6. greenhouse 7. allow   8. crawl
9. unlike 10. short   11. endanger 12. digest

B
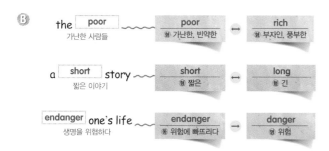

C 1. nutrients   2. short   3. greenhouse 4. allow

D 1. unlike   2. crawl   3. wide   4. digest
5. poor   6. endangers   7. mysterious 8. If

E The Venus Flytrap   p.77

The Venus flytrap is a **mysterious** plant.
<u>Unlike</u> other plants, it is an insect-eating plant.
It gets <u>nutrients</u> from eating insects like ants, flies, or spiders.
The Venus flytrap lives in **poor** conditions in North and South Carolina.
People collect so many Venus flytraps that they have become **endangered**.
So they are grown in <u>greenhouses</u> today.
The leaves of the Venus flytrap are usually open <u>wide</u>.
<u>Short</u> hairs cover the leaves.
When an insect <u>crawls</u> on its leaves, its leaves close quickly.
The hairs and leaves don't <u>allow</u> the insect to escape.
The Venus flytrap **digests** the soft, inner parts of the insect.
<u>If</u> it swallows a stone or a nut, the leaves reopen and spit it out.
This is the way the Venus flytrap lives.

● 해석 ●

파리지옥

파리지옥은 신비로운 식물이다.
다른 식물들과는 달리 이것은 곤충을 잡아먹는 식물이다.
이것은 개미, 파리 또는 거미와 같은 곤충들을 먹어서 영양분을 섭취한다.
파리지옥은 북남부 캐롤라이나의 척박한 조건에서 산다.
사람들이 너무 많은 파리지옥을 채집하는 바람에 그것들은 위험에 처하게 되었다.
그래서 그것들은 오늘날 온실에서 길러진다.
파리지옥의 잎들은 보통 활짝 열려 있다.
짧은 털들이 잎을 덮고 있다.
곤충이 잎 위를 기어 다니면 잎들이 재빨리 잎을 닫는다.
털들과 잎은 곤충이 탈출하는 것을 허용하지 않는다.
파리지옥은 곤충의 부드러운 안쪽 부분을 소화한다.
만약 파리지옥이 돌이나 견과류를 삼키면 잎들은 다시 잎을 열고 이것을 뱉어낸다.
이것이 파리지옥이 살아가는 방법이다.

• Lesson 2 • A Helpful Plant   p.78

A 1. die   2. tickle   3. side   4. helpful
5. get rid of 6. solution   7. key   8. gather
9. troublesome 10. shovel   11. swamp
12. lose

B 1. gather   2. get rid of 3. helpful   4. key

C

D 1. swamp   2. helpful   3. die   4. troublesome
5. get rid of 6. key   7. gather   8. solution
9. tickles   10. lose my footing   11. shovel
12. side

E A Helpful Plant   p.81

Nick and his friends <u>gather</u> at Michelle's house.
Fruit flies are flying around them.
"How can we <u>get rid of</u> these fruit flies? They're **troublesome**."
Michelle says, "I have a <u>solution</u>. A Venus flytrap is the **key**. Let's get a Venus flytrap."
They go to a <u>swamp</u> where the Venus flytrap grows.
Nick finds a Venus flytrap. It looks different from other

Venus flytraps. It's very big.

At that moment, he <u>loses</u> <u>his</u> <u>footing</u> and slips.

"Look! The big Venus flytrap is swallowing Nick," cries Michelle.

"Pull the <u>sides</u> of the leaves. Hurry," shouts Grace.

Grace and Michelle try to open its leaves.

"I'm going to <u>tickle</u> it," says Justin.

The Venus flytrap spits Nick out.

"Whew~! I almost <u>died</u>," says Nick.

They dig it out with a <u>shovel</u> and take it to Michelle's house.

The Venus flytrap catches all the fruit flies at Michelle's house.

What a <u>helpful</u> plant!

● 해석 ●

유용한 식물

닉과 그의 친구들이 미셸의 집에 모인다.
초파리들이 그들 주위를 날아다닌다.
"어떻게 이 초파리들을 없앨 수 있을까? 이것들은 골칫덩어리야."
미셸이 말한다. "나에게 해결책이 있어. 파리지옥이 바로 그 비결이지. 파리지옥을 가지러 가자."
그들은 파리지옥이 사는 늪으로 간다.
닉이 파리지옥을 발견한다. 그것은 다른 파리지옥들과 달라 보인다. 그것은 아주 크다.
그 순간, 그는 발을 헛디뎌 미끄러진다.
"여길 봐! 큰 파리지옥이 닉을 삼키고 있어." 미셸이 소리지른다.
"잎의 양쪽을 잡아당겨. 서둘러." 그레이스가 소리친다.
그레이스와 미셸이 잎을 열려고 노력한다.
"내가 이것을 간질일게."라고 저스틴이 말한다.
파리지옥이 닉을 뱉어 낸다.
닉이 말한다. "휴~! 거의 죽을 뻔했어."
그들은 삽으로 그것을 파내서 미셸의 집으로 가지고 온다.
파리지옥이 미셸의 집에서 모든 초파리들을 잡는다.
정말 유용한 식물이다!

Unit 10

The Guinness Book
기네스북

• Lesson 1 • **A Guinness World Record** p.82

Ⓐ 1. apply   2. now   3. dwarves   4. Who
5. hugest   6. send   7. cockroach   8. fact
9. measure   10. detail   11. record   12. the same

Ⓑ

huge – hugest
거대한 – 가장 거대한

long – longest
긴 – 가장 긴

fast – fastest
빠른 – 가장 빠른

small 형 작은	→	smallest 형 가장 작은
light 형 가벼운	→	lightest 형 가장 가벼운
tall 형 키 큰	→	tallest 형 가장 키가 큰

Ⓒ 1. cockroaches   2. send   3. now   4. detail

Ⓓ 1. Who   2. dwarves   3. measure   4. fact
5. hugest   6. applied   7. the same, as
8. break, record

Ⓔ **A Guinness World Record**   p.85

How big is the <u>hugest</u> pizza in the world?

It is about 37.4 m. That is <u>the</u> <u>same</u> size <u>as</u> a 10-story building.

How small is the smallest <u>cockroach</u> in the world?

A cockroach in Japan <u>measured</u> 9 mm long.

<u>Who</u> is the world's lightest person?

It is a Mexican <u>dwarf</u>, who is 67 cm tall and weighs 2.14 kg.

We can find these <u>facts</u> in the Guinness Book of World Records.

It is a popular book that <u>details</u> the world's new records.

Does anyone want to <u>break</u> <u>a</u> world <u>record</u>?

Try and then <u>apply</u> for a Guinness world record.

<u>Send</u> your new record to the Guinness book.

Try it <u>now</u>.

● 해석 ●

기네스 세계 기록

세계에서 가장 거대한 피자는 얼마나 클까?
그것은 약 37.4 미터이다. 10층 높이 건물과 같은 크기이다.
세계에서 가장 작은 바퀴벌레는 얼마나 작을까?
일본에 있는 바퀴벌레는 9 밀리미터였다.
세계에서 가장 가벼운 사람은 누굴까?
멕시코 난쟁이인데, 67 센티미터의 키에 2.14 킬로그램이다.
우리는 이러한 사실들을 세계 기네스북에서 찾을 수 있다.
이것은 세계의 새로운 기록들을 상세하게 보여 주는 인기 있는 책이다.
세계 기록을 깨고 싶은 사람이 있는가?
시도해 보고 기네스 세계 기록에 신청해라.
당신의 새로운 기록을 기네스북에 보내라.
지금 해봐라.

• Lesson 2 • **Nick's World Record** p.86

Ⓐ 1. medicine　2. continued　3. beef　　4. upset
　5. sore　　6. tie　　　7. blame　　8. chalk
　9. disappoint　10. in class　11. button up　12. fall off

Ⓑ 1. tie　　　2. button up　3. fell off

Ⓒ

　동 화나게 하다 ——————• You upset me.
　　　　　　　　　　　　　네가 나를 화나게 한다

　형 속상한　　　• I have an upset stomach.
　　　　　　　　　　나는 위가 탈이 났다.

　형 탈이 난　　　• He was upset about his brother's
　　　　　　　　　　bad behaviour.
　　　　　　　　　　그는 남동생의 나쁜 행동에 ___속상___ 했다.

Ⓓ 1. fell off　　2. sore　　3. buttons up　4. beef
　5. medicine　6. chalk　　7. in class　　8. upset
　9. tie　　　10. disappointed　　11. blame
　12. continue

Ⓔ **Nick's World Record**　p.89

Nick wants to break a Guinness world record.
Nick tries eating <u>beef</u> as fast as he can.
He has an <u>upset</u> stomach. So he takes some <u>medicine</u>.
Nick practices throwing **chalk** as far as he can.
He gets punished by his teacher for throwing chalk <u>in class</u>.
Nick tries to **button up** his clothes quickly.
His mom <u>blames</u> him because all of the buttons on his clothes <u>fall off</u>.
He tries to <u>tie</u> his shoes the fastest.
He gives up because his hands are <u>sore</u>.
Nick's really **disappointed**. But Nick never gives up.
Nick will <u>continue</u> to try to set a world record.

● 해석 ●
닉의 세계 기록
닉은 기네스 세계 기록을 깨고 싶다.
닉은 소고기 최대한 빨리 먹기를 시도한다.
그는 배탈이 난다. 그래서 약을 좀 먹는다.
닉은 분필을 최대한 멀리 던지는 연습을 한다.
그는 수업 중에 분필을 던져서 선생님께 혼이 난다.
닉은 옷 단추 빨리 잠그기를 해본다.
그의 엄마는 닉의 옷에서 단추들이 모두 떨어져서 그를 혼낸다.
그는 신발 끈을 가장 빨리 묶는 것을 해본다.
그는 손이 아파서 포기한다.
닉은 정말 실망한다. 하지만 닉은 결코 포기하지 않는다.
닉은 세계 기록을 세우려고 계속 시도할 것이다.

WoW! Smart Vocabulary

보너스 지식이 팡팡!
케이블카 타는 것보다 재미있는
블루베리 껌보다 맛있는 책 (이혜린 서현초 3학년)
러(너)와 나 함께
리(이)야기 속 단어 공부 여행 떠나보자
(임서영 탄천초 4학년)

보면 신나는 지식
케이스에 소중하게 담아두는 지식
블럭처럼 쌓아가는 우리의 지식 (장서연 서현초 3학년)
러(너)와 나의 지식이야
리(이) 책을 펼쳐봐, 엄청난 지식이 쏟아질 거야
(황인태 서현초 3학년)

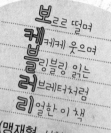

와우, 영어 공부 하기에 정말 좋아요
우와, 더욱 자세히 나와 있네요
스마트한 영어 공부법
마트에는 없어요~ 서점으로 오세요
트러블이 영어이신 분, 이제 쉽게 공부할 수 있어요
(박지수 용마초 5학년)

보르르 떨며
케케케 웃으며
블링블링 있는
러브레터처럼
리얼한 이 책
(맹재형 서현초 3학년)

보아야 후회 안 되는
케잡처럼 톡톡 튀는 (천사랑 용마초 5학년)
블럭 버스터의 숨막히는 장면처럼
러블리한 영어 단어들
리(이)야기로 공부하면 모두 내 것이 되지
(장우혁 탄천초 6학년)

와우~ 재미있는 이야기가 가득!
우리들이 쉽게 읽을 수 있는 즐거운 스토리
스마트한 영단어를
마구마구 쏙쏙 집어넣은 이야기
트집잡을 게 없는 완벽한 교재야!
(민동안 용마초 6학년)

보물섬 같은 영어의 세계
케케묵은 단어 외우기 공부 말고
블랙홀처럼 모든 단어를 빨아들이는 방법 없을까?
러(너)무 고민하지마~
리(이) 책으로
이야기와 함께 공부하면 고민 해결!
(신하진 탄천초 4학년)

보고 또 봐도 질리지 않고
케이크처럼 달고
블루베리보다 좋아 (박정은 서현초 3학년)
러브하고 싶을 정도
리(이)렇게 재미있는 책은 처음이에요
(손효민 서현초 3학년)